Go Figure!

Exploring Figurative Language

the early bird catches the worm

Move at a Snail's Pace

time is money

Timothy Rasinski, Ph.D.
Jerry Zutell, Ph.D.
Melissa Cheesman Smith, M.Ed.

Publishing Credits

Corinne Burton, M.A.Ed., *President;* Conni Medina, M.A.Ed., *Managing Editor ;* Emily Smith, M.A.Ed., *Content Director;* Angela Johnson-Rogers, M.F.A., M.S.Ed., *Editor;* Lee Aucoin, *Senior Graphic Designer;* Kevin Pham, *Graphic Designer;* Kyleena Harper, *Assistant Editor*

Image Credits

All images from iStock and Shutterstock.

Standards

© Copyright 2010. National Governors Association Center for Best Practices and Council of Chief State School Officers. All rights reserved.

Shell Education

A division of Teacher Created Materials
5301 Oceanus Drive
Huntington Beach, CA 92649-1030

http://www.tcmpub.com/shell-education

ISBN 978-1-4258-1625-4

©2017 Shell Education Publishing, Inc.

Table of Contents

Introduction and Research

Figurative language is embedded in both written and oral language across all content areas. Familiarizing students with common figures of speech enables them to better understand the world around them in their reading and their social encounters. Figures of speech are a fun way to engage students with phrases in your classroom through bulletin boards, interactive activities, and social speech opportunities.

The overarching term *figurative language* encompasses words or phrases that mean something more or different from their literal definitions. Figurative language includes words used in nonliteral ways through different figures of speech for the purposes of enhancing language and making it livelier. There are many types of figures of speech in the English language, including idioms, proverbs, similes, metaphors, personification, hyperbole, and oxymorons. (See page 7 for more information on the types of figures of speech.) Inferred meaning of a figurative phrase is not something that students learn by dissecting the individual words. Rather, students must study and understand the context of the words or phrases through reading, social speech, and cultural experiences.

This series was designed to make this important part of word study interactive and relevant for students. So, when it comes to teaching vocabulary, don't *sit on the fence*, don't *have cold feet*, and don't *try to pull any strings*. Let us do the honors and *make heads or tails* out of teaching figurative language for your students. Before you know it, you'll be *standing on your own two feet* and teaching figurative language will be *as comfortable as an old shoe*. Moreover, your students will *fall head over heels* in love with figurative language as they read and write.

"Literal" vs. "Figurative"

Figurative meanings are often quite different from the literal meanings. The *literal* meaning of a figure of speech means exactly what each word says. The *figurative* meaning of a figure of speech *implies* or *infers* what the phrase together says in a different way, more than the surface or literal meaning.

Content-Area Themes

When teachers merge literacy into content-area learning, students' vocabularies are improved in positive ways. While figures of speech are not meant to directly teach content, the meanings of the words relate to the content the students are learning and allow students to see how words can play on each other, often through multiple meanings.

Effective teachers can connect literacy to the content areas, which makes for authentic practice and learning. By studying figurative language, and specifically idioms and proverbs, within the content areas, students can associate these figures of speech to academic vocabulary and words they hear in science, social studies, and mathematics. This book is divided into content-area themes so students can connect learning about these idioms and proverbs to content-area vocabulary.

Introduction and Research (cont.)

Why Is Figurative Language Important?

Figurative language is part and parcel of oral and written language. Use of figures of speech goes back thousands of years and allows writing to come alive in creative and engaging ways. English is rich in idioms (Harris and Hodges 1995), an important type of figurative language. Since English is filled with such language, it can be a challenge to understand (Blachowicz and Fisher 2014). This is especially true for English language learners who have had even less exposure to experiences involving the figurative meanings of phrases in the English language.

Every learner comes across figurative language that can be difficult to understand because they have not been previously exposed to the figures of speech and/or were not told the meanings or given sufficient clues to make sense of the figurative implications of the words. Children, by their very nature of having limited life experiences, are more likely to encounter figurative language they do not understand. Struggling readers have special difficulty with figurative language because they lack textual experience with it and because their focus tends to be on unlocking the pronunciations of individual words and accessing their literal meanings. English language learners have special difficulty with figurative language because of a lack of English experience and because idioms rarely translate directly from one language to another. Therefore, teachers need to spend time explicitly teaching figurative language in the classroom.

The use of figurative language in writing is a characteristic of high-quality literature (Blachowicz and Fisher 2014). Authors include idioms and proverbs in their writing to clarify their messages and make the writing more interesting to readers. Blachowicz and Fisher (2014) argue that authors use figurative language, including unusual juxtapositions of words, to draw attention to and enlighten us about various aspects of our world. However, if a reader is unfamiliar with the figurative phrase in the text, then he or she is likely to have a poor or limited understanding of those aspects.

Research indicates that children understand relatively simple figures of speech in familiar contexts (e.g., similes and metaphors). As text increases in difficulty, the figures of speech being used become less familiar and more complex. Thus, figurative language can contribute to difficulty in comprehension of rigorous texts. This book focuses on some of those items less familiar to children, especially in the form of idioms and proverbs.

The Importance of Figurative Language

- Figurative language saturates the English language.

- Figurative language has a major impact on written and oral comprehension.

- Figurative language adds a richness, color, and creativity to reading, writing, and thinking.

Introduction and Research *(cont.)*

The Importance of Studying Figures of Speech

The National Reading Panel (2000) has identified vocabulary as an essential component of effective literacy instruction. When students do not know the meanings of the words and phrases in the texts they read, they are likely to experience difficulty in sufficiently understanding those same texts. Some of the most difficult sentences to understand contain words and phrases that are not meant to express their literal meanings but their figurative ones.

Figures of speech are found everywhere. Students need to be exposed to many different figures of speech for general cultural awareness and to develop an understanding that not all words and expressions are meant to be taken literally. Thus, the study of figurative language is certainly worthwhile, as great awareness and understanding of such language structures can enhance students' understanding of the texts they read. Despite the fact that today's college and career readiness standards recognize the importance of studying figurative language, most core reading or language arts curricular programs do not provide adequate instructional coverage of figurative language. Therefore, the *Go Figure! Exploring Figurative Language* series provides specific and engaging instruction on figurative language for students. As students become more acquainted with figurative language, reading comprehension and written composition will improve.

The major intent of this series is to improve students' reading comprehension and overall reading achievement. However, as noted earlier, high-quality writing is marked by the use of figurative language. Thus, improving students' writing skills is very likely to be a secondary benefit of using *Go Figure! Exploring Figurative Language*. As students' knowledge and use of figurative language improves and expands, the quality of their writing will likely show measurable gains as well.

Steps to Introduce Figures of Speech

1. Read the figure of speech.
2. Think about the literal meaning of the phrase.
3. Predict the figurative meaning of the phrase.
4. Use resources to discover the meaning of the figure of speech.
5. Read the figure of speech in context, as it might be used in the text.
6. Talk about why an author might choose this figure of speech and how it would affect the overall meaning of the text.

Introduction and Research *(cont.)*

Definitions of Selected Figures of Speech

It's easy to confuse the various types of figurative language. Although all these types of figures of speech are not used in the book, this chart serves as a good reference for you and your students.

	Definition	Example
allusion	referring to a person, place, or thing without mentioning it directly	She acted like a *Scrooge*.
euphemism	the substitution of a mild or pleasant word for one considered offensive	The family dog *passed away*.
hyperbole	an exaggerated statement	I'm so hungry *I could eat a horse*!
idiom	a phrase that means something very different from the literal meaning	He was *as hungry as a bear*.
irony	a statement or situation that is the opposite of what you expect	That's as strange as *a pilot with a fear of heights*.
metaphor	a direct comparison between two unlike things	The *moon is a mirror*.
oxymoron	contradictory terms that appear side by side	The guilty pet sat in *deafening silence* as her owner cleaned up the kitchen.
paradox	a statement that appears to contradict itself	The story was *bittersweet*.
personification	an inanimate object is given human qualities	*The angry sea seethed endlessly.*
proverb	a memorable saying based on facts and generally thought to be true	*Do unto others as you want done unto you.*
pun	a play on words	Fish are *smart* because they live in *schools*.
simile	a comparison (usually formed with "like" or "as") between two things	Her eyes were *as bright as the sun*.

How to Use This Series

Activity Descriptions

Teacher Overview Page

Purpose: This page provides organization for each unit. On this page you will find the following:

1. The five figurative phrases used in the unit
2. Additional figures of speech for the theme
3. Answers for each lesson in the unit
4. Overview materials needed for the lessons in the unit

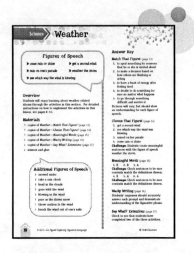

Match That Figure!

Purpose: Provide definitions and orient students to the meaning of each figure of speech.

Preparation: Copy this page with nothing on the back, as it will be cut at the bottom.

Procedure

1. Have students cut apart the definitions at the bottom of the page.
2. Explain each figure of speech while students glue each card next to its corresponding figure of speech. Or, allow students to match the definitions with the figures of speech first and then discuss them.
3. Tell students to draw pictures to help them remember the figurative meanings of the figures of speech.
4. This sheet is great for students to reference while completing the other activities.

Choose That Figure!

Purpose: Allow students to practice using the figures of speech in context.

Preparation: Copy the activity page and distribute to students.

Procedure

1. Have students read each sentence provided and choose the figure of speech that best completes each sentence.
2. At the end, have students create their own sentences using the figure of speech not used in one of the previous sentences. (If a student chooses an incorrect figure of speech in a previous sentence and then writes a sentence with the wrong figure of speech, he or she should still be given credit for the correct sentence.)

How to Use This Series (cont.)

Activity Descriptions (cont.)

Meaningful Words

Purpose: Provide exploration of multiple meanings of words in context. **Note:** Sometimes, the words will have very close meanings but are different parts of speech. For example, students may have to choose between "doctor" as a person or an action. This helps students pay attention to detail and use familiar words in new ways.

Preparation: Copy the activity page or display it for the class to view.

Procedure

1. For each activity set, have students read the chosen word and review the different meanings of the word. **Note:** Specific definitions were chosen for each word but not every common definition was used.
2. Have students choose which definition matches how the word is used in the context of each sentence. Students can underline or highlight which words they used as context clues to aid in choosing a definition.
3. For the challenge activity, students choose one definition and write a sentence that correctly shows context for the meaning of the word with the chosen definition.

Wacky Writing

Purpose: Practice the meanings of the figures of speech through application in writing.

Preparation: Copy the activity page or display it for the class to view.

Procedure

1. Have students read and answer each prompt.
2. Answers will vary, and correct completion is based on correct application of the figure of speech in the answer.

How to Use This Series (cont.)

Activity Descriptions (cont.)

Say What? Extensions

Purpose: Apply knowledge of the figures of speech through critical thinking, language practice, and creativity during challenging and fun activities.

Preparation: Read each activity ahead of time to determine what supplies the students may need, and have these supplies available to the students (e.g., flashcards, markers).

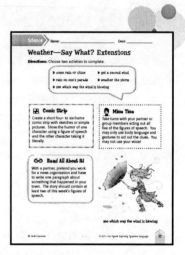

Procedure

1. Have students select and complete two of the three activities provided. Some activities are completed individually, while others are completed with partners or in small groups.
2. **Optional**: You may decide to have students choose only one activity, or complete all activities if time permits.

Correlation to the Standards

Shell Education is committed to producing educational materials that are research and standards based. As part of this effort, we have correlated all of our products to the academic standards of all 50 states, the District of Columbia, the Department of Defense Dependents Schools, and all Canadian provinces.

Purpose and Intent of Standards

The Every Student Succeeds Act (ESSA) mandates that all states adopt challenging academic standards that help students meet the goal of college and career readiness. While many states already adopted academic standards prior to ESSA, the act continues to hold states accountable for detailed and comprehensive standards. Standards are statements that describe the criteria necessary for students to meet specific academic goals. They define the knowledge, skills, and content students should acquire at each level. State standards are used in the development of our products, so educators can be assured they meet state academic requirements.

How to Find Standards Correlations

To print a customized correlation report of this product for your state, visit our website at **www.teachercreatedmaterials.com/administrators/correlations/** and follow the online directions. If you require assistance in printing correlation reports, please contact our Customer Service Department at 1-877-777-3450.

How to Use This Series (cont.)

Extension Activities Descriptions

Each extension activity focuses on one type of learning: visual, kinesthetic, auditory, linguistic, spatial, intrapersonal, or interpersonal. This chart explains each extension activity in this book.

Extension	Type of Learning	Explanation
Comic Strip	visual	Create a comic strip to demonstrate the humor of misunderstanding a figure of speech and how that can lead to confusion.
Critical Thinking	kinesthetic	Use sketches to have friends guess each figure of speech.
Drive Me Crazy!	auditory	Use the phrase *drive you to the edge* in everyday situations.
Example and Non-example	linguistic	To gain a better understanding of meaning, think, write, and discuss examples and non-examples of the figures of speech.
Figurative and Literal	kinesthetic	Using creativity, draw a literal and figurative interpretation of the figurative phrase.
Fishing for a Compliment	kinesthetic	Show comprehension of the phrase *fishing for a compliment* by writing compliments to people in the real world.
Floating on Air	intrapersonal	Apply the meaning of *floating on air* to a personal experience.
Hands in Motion	kinesthetic	Use hand motions to show comprehension of each figure of speech in a social context.
I'm the Judge	interpersonal	Apply the meaning of the figurative phrase *you can't judge a book by its cover* to the real world.
Look Like a Million Bucks	spatial	Show creativity and understanding of the phrase *looked like a million bucks* through discussion.
Matching Game	kinesthetic	Practice matching each definition to its corresponding phrase in a fun and engaging way.
Memory Game	kinesthetic	Test memory and understanding of the figures of speech by using index cards to paraphrase the definitions.
Mime Time	kinesthetic	Use body language and gestures to show comprehension of the figures of speech.
Poetry Time	musical, linguistic	Create a rhyming poem, verse, or song to define each figure of speech.
Read All About It!	auditory, linguistic	Write a creative short story for a newspaper using at least two figures of speech.
Say It, Don't Spray It!	linguistic	Write a short story using all the figures of speech.
Short Story	linguistic	Use at least two figures of speech to write a personal story.
Sing Me a Song	musical, linguistic	Use a familiar musical beat or tempo to construct a song using a figure of speech.
Tell Me a Tale	linguistic	Construct a fairy tale using multiple figures of speech.
Wrong Side of the Law	linguistic	Use the phrase *took the law into your hands* to explain a historical event.

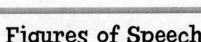

Figures of Speech

» come rain or shine   » get a second wind

» rain on one's parade   » weather the storm

» see which way the wind is blowing

Overview

Students will enjoy learning about weather-related idioms through the activities in this section. For detailed instructions on how to implement the activities in this lesson, see pages 8–10.

Materials

> copies of *Weather—Match That Figure!* (page 13)
> copies of *Weather—Choose That Figure!* (page 14)
> copies of *Weather—Meaningful Words* (page 15)
> copies of *Weather—Wacky Writing* (page 16)
> copies of *Weather—Say What? Extensions* (page 17)
> scissors and glue

Additional Figures of Speech

> snowed under
> take a rain check
> head in the clouds
> gone with the wind
> blowing in the wind
> pure as the driven snow
> throw caution to the wind
> knock the wind out of one's sails

Answer Key

Match That Figure! (page 13)

1. to spoil something for someone that he or she is excited about
2. to make a decision based on how others are thinking or acting
3. to have a burst of energy after feeling tired
4. to decide to do something for sure no matter what happens
5. to go through something difficult and survive it

Pictures will vary, but should show an understanding for each figure of speech.

Choose That Figure! (page 14)

1. got a second wind
2. see which way the wind was blowing
3. rained on her parade
4. come rain or shine

Challenge: Students create meaningful sentences with the figure of speech *weather the storm*.

Meaningful Words (page 15)

1. B   2. B   3. A

Challenge: Check sentences to be sure contexts match the definitions chosen.

4. B   5. A   6. A

Challenge: Check sentences to be sure contexts match the definitions chosen.

Wacky Writing (page 16)

Students' responses should accurately answer each prompt and demonstrate understanding of the figurative phrase.

Say What? Extensions (page 17)

Check to see that students have completed two of the three activities.

Science　Name _____　Date _____

Weather—Match That Figure!

Directions: Cut apart the definition cards. Glue each definition next to the correct phrase. Then, draw a picture to represent each figurative phrase.

Phrases	Definitions	Pictures
1. rain on one's parade		
2. see which way the wind is blowing		
3. get a second wind		
4. come rain or shine		
5. weather the storm		

to have a burst of energy after feeling tired	to spoil something for someone that he or she is excited about	to go through something difficult and survive it	to decide to do something for sure no matter what happens	to make a decision based on how others are thinking or acting

Weather—Choose That Figure!

Directions: Write the correct figure of speech in each sentence.

> » come rain or shine   » got a second wind
>
> » rained on her parade   » weather the storm
>
> » see which way the wind was blowing

1. After a long day at school, Tiana _____

   _____ and wanted to go ride her bike outside.

2. Gene checked to _____

   _____ before he decided how to present his science project.

3. Zara was excited about her award, but Jill _____

   _____ when she half-heartedly congratulated her.

4. Dad shouted, "_____

   _____ , we are going to finish painting the cupboards today!"

Challenge: Write a sentence using the figure of speech not used above.

_____

_____

_____

_____

_____

Weather—Meaningful Words

Directions: For each sentence, write the letter of the correct definition. Then, create your own sentence using the selected word.

come rain or <u>shine</u>	A. shine (verb): to give out light B. shine (verb): to do really well at something

_____ 1. Pablo didn't play sports well, but he shined in mathematics.

_____ 2. Maria shined during her choir performance.

_____ 3. Her new diamond shined as she showed it off to the cameras.

Challenge: Choose a definition, and write a sentence using the word *shine*.

_____

_____

weather the <u>storm</u>	A. storm (noun): weather with heavy winds, rain or snow B. storm (verb): to feel and show angry emotion

_____ 4. Jeff knew his boss was angry, after she stormed out of the office.

_____ 5. The storm caused damage to the roof of the house.

_____ 6. We got our flashlights when the storm caused the electricity to go out.

Challenge: Choose a definition, and write a sentence using the word *storm*.

_____

_____

Weather—Wacky Writing

Directions: Read and answer each prompt.

1. Describe one goal you know you will achieve one day, *come rain or shine.*

    _____

    _____

    _____

2. Describe a time when you waited to *see which way the wind was blowing* before making a decision.

    _____

    _____

3. Describe a time when someone *rained on your parade.* How did you feel?

    _____

    _____

    _____

4. List three things you can do to calm yourself down when things get difficult and you need to *weather the storm.*

    _____

    _____

5. Explain what time of day you are most likely to need *a second wind.* Why?

    _____

    _____

    _____

Weather—Say What? Extensions

Directions: Choose two activities to complete.

> » come rain or shine   » get a second wind
>
> » rain on one's parade   » weather the storm
>
> » see which way the wind is blowing

Comic Strip

Create a short four- to six-frame comic strip with sketches or simple pictures. Show the humor of one character using a figure of speech and the other character taking it literally.

👤 Mime Time

Take turns with your partner or group members acting out all five of the figures of speech. You may only use body language and gestures to act out the clues. You may not use your voice!

👓 Read All About It!

With a partner, pretend you work for a news organization and have to write one paragraph about something that happened in your town. The story should contain at least two of this week's figures of speech.

see which way the wind is blowing

51625—Go Figure! Exploring Figurative Language

Figures of Speech

» ants in your pants   » move at a snail's pace

» bitten by the same bug   » snug as a bug in a rug

» butterflies in your stomach

Overview

Students will enjoy learning about bug- and insect-related idioms through the activities in this section. For detailed instructions on how to implement the activities in this lesson, see pages 8–10.

Materials

› copies of *Bugs and Insects—Match That Figure!* (page 19)

› copies of *Bugs and Insects—Choose That Figure!* (page 20)

› copies of *Bugs and Insects—Meaningful Words* (page 21)

› copies of *Bugs and Insects—Wacky Writing* (page 22)

› copies of *Bugs and Insects—Say What? Extensions* (page 23)

› scissors and glue

› index cards

Additional Figures of Speech

› bug off

› bug-eyed

› don't bug me

› a bee in your bonnet

› put a bug in your ear

› making one's skin crawl

› wouldn't hurt a flea

Answer Key

Match That Figure! (page 19)
1. nervous and moving around a lot
2. wrapped up tight, warm, and comfortable
3. feeling nervous about doing something
4. having the same desire, need, or idea
5. to move or do a task at a really slow pace

Pictures will vary, but should show an understanding for each figure of speech.

Choose That Figure! (page 20)
1. butterflies in her stomach
2. snug as a bug in a rug
3. ants in her pants
4. moved at a snail's pace

Challenge: Students create meaningful sentences with the figure of speech *bitten by the same bug*.

Meaningful Words (page 21)
1. B   2. B   3. A

Challenge: Check sentences to be sure contexts match the definitions chosen.
4. B   5. A   6. A

Challenge: Check sentences to be sure contexts match the definitions chosen.

Wacky Writing (page 22)
Students' responses should accurately answer each prompt and demonstrate understanding of the figurative phrase.

Say What? Extensions (page 23)
Check to see that students have completed two of the three activities.

Bugs and Insects—Match That Figure!

Directions: Cut apart the definition cards. Glue each definition next to the correct phrase. Then, draw a picture to represent each figurative phrase.

Phrases	Definitions	Pictures
1. ants in your pants		
2. snug as a bug in a rug		
3. butterflies in your stomach		
4. bitten by the same bug		
5. move at a snail's pace		

feeling nervous about doing something	to move or do a task at a really slow pace	nervous and moving around a lot	having the same desire, need, or idea	wrapped up tight, warm, and comfortable

Bugs and Insects—Choose That Figure!

Directions: Write the correct figure of speech in each sentence.

> » ants in her pants   » moved at snail's pace
>
> » bitten by the same bug   » snug as a bug in a rug
>
> » butterflies in her stomach

1. Christie felt like she had _____

   _____ because she had to give a speech in front of her class.

2. Mario's father tucks him in and makes sure he is _____

   _____ each night.

3. Jacqueline felt like she had _____

   _____ while waiting to go out to recess.

4. Jeremiah was dreading pulling weeds in the backyard after school, so he

   _____ while walking home.

Challenge: Write a sentence using the figure of speech not used above.

_____

_____

_____

_____

Bugs and Insects—Meaningful Words

Directions: For each sentence, write the letter of the correct definition. Then, create your own sentence using the selected word.

bitten by the same <u>bug</u>	A. bug (noun): an insect B. bug (verb): to bother or annoy

_____ 1. The kids bugged us by talking through the whole movie.

_____ 2. Alberto loved to bug his sister whenever she was reading.

_____ 3. Dad screamed when he saw the bug in the bathroom.

Challenge: Choose a definition, and write a sentence using the word *bug*.

_____

_____

<u>move</u> at a snail's pace	A. move (verb): to be in one place/position, then go to another B. move (verb): having an emotional response to something

_____ 4. The girls were so moved by the beautiful performance that they cried.

_____ 5. Salma's dad got a new job, so they had to move to California.

_____ 6. James moved around a lot in his seat while he was working at his desk.

Challenge: Choose a definition, and write a sentence using the word *move*.

_____

_____

Name _____ Date _____

Bugs and Insects—Wacky Writing

Directions: Read and answer each prompt.

1. Describe something you would be *bitten by the same bug* to do if your friend got you excited about it.

   _____

   _____

2. List three things that might make you have *butterflies in your stomach* if you had to do them.

   _____

   _____

3. Name three things you can do to use up your energy if you have *ants in your pants*.

   _____

   _____

4. Describe a time you would want to *move at a snail's pace*.

   _____

   _____

   _____

5. Explain why you do or do not like to be wrapped up in a blanket *snug as a bug in a rug*.

   _____

   _____

   _____

51625—Go Figure! Exploring Figurative Language   © Shell Education

Bugs and Insects—Say What? Extensions

Directions: Choose two activities to complete.

> » ants in your pants   » move at a snail's pace
>
> » bitten by the same bug   » snug as a bug in a rug
>
> » butterflies in your stomach

◀▶ Matching Game

Create a matching game with a partner. Using 10 index cards, write each figure of speech on one card and your own definition for each phrase on another card. Mix up all the cards. Time how long it takes you to match each figure of speech with its definition. Have your partner try to beat your time. Each person goes twice to see who can achieve the fastest time.

Critical Thinking

Create a piece of artwork with symbols and pictures that represent the meaning of one of the figures of speech. You may not use any words in the piece. Share your picture with a partner or group to see if they can guess which figure of speech you chose.

Sing Me a Song

With a partner, write a simple song to a familiar tune. Include at least one of the figures of speech in your song. Share your song by singing it or reading the lyrics aloud like a poem.

ants in your pants

Figures of Speech

» bloom where you are planted   » plant a seed

» sow seeds of kindness   » turn over a new leaf

» don't let the grass grow under your feet

Overview

Students will enjoy learning about plant- and growing-related idioms through the activities in this section. For detailed instructions on how to implement the activities in this lesson, see pages 8–10.

Materials

> copies of *Plants and Growing—Match That Figure!* (page 25)

> copies of *Plants and Growing—Choose That Figure!* (page 26)

> copies of *Plants and Growing—Meaningful Words* (page 27)

> copies of *Plants and Growing—Wacky Writing* (page 28)

> copies of *Plants and Growing—Say What? Extensions* (page 29)

> scissors and glue

> index cards

Additional Figures of Speech

> leaf through a book

> grow by leaps and bounds

> take a leaf out of someone's book

> absence makes the heart grow fonder

Answer Key

Match That Figure! (page 25)

1. do something now that will help something develop in the future
2. do something kind to cause other people to be kind
3. try and do a good job in the place or situation you are currently in
4. don't stay in one place too long, get going and make progress
5. to begin anew and get rid of bad habits

Pictures will vary, but should show an understanding for each figure of speech.

Choose That Figure! (page 26)

1. bloom where he was planted
2. let the grass grow under his feet
3. sowing seeds of kindness
4. turn over a new leaf

Challenge: Students create meaningful sentences with the figure of speech *plant a seed.*

Meaningful Words (page 27)

1. C   2. B   3. A

Challenge: Check sentences to be sure contexts match the definitions chosen.

4. A   5. A   6. B

Challenge: Check sentences to be sure contexts match the definitions chosen.

Wacky Writing (page 28)

Students' responses should accurately answer each prompt and demonstrate understanding of the figurative phrase.

Say What? Extensions (page 29)

Check to see that students have completed two of the three activities.

Plants and Growing—Match That Figure!

Directions: Cut apart the definition cards. Glue each definition next to the correct phrase. Then, draw a picture to represent each figurative phrase.

Phrases	Definitions	Pictures
1. plant a seed		
2. sow seeds of kindness		
3. bloom where you are planted		
4. don't let the grass grow under your feet		
5. turn over a new leaf		

try and do a good job in the place or situation you are currently in	don't stay in one place too long, get going and make progress	do something now that will help something develop in the future	to begin anew and get rid of bad habits	do something kind to cause other people to be kind

Plants and Growing—Choose That Figure!

Directions: Write the correct figure of speech in each sentence.

> » bloom where he was planted   » plant a seed
>
> » sowing seeds of kindness   » turn over a new leaf
>
> »let the grass grow under his feet

1. Even though Dennis wasn't interested in volleyball, he decided to _____

   _____ and do his best.

2. Mr. Creed told his son not to _____

   _____ and get to work on his homework.

3. Olivia had many friends because she was always _____

   _____ .

4. Troy often kept his room messy, but starting in the New Year he decided to

   _____ and keep it clean without reminders.

Challenge: Write a sentence using the figure of speech not used above.

_____

_____

_____

_____

Plants and Growing—Meaningful Words

Directions: For each sentence, write the letter of the correct definition. Then, create your own sentence using the selected word.

<u>plant</u> a seed	**A.** plant (noun): a living sprout that grows from earth and requires sun and water to live
	B. plant (noun): a factory or workshop
	C. plant (verb): to put seeds in the ground for growth

_____ 1. Ellie planted the leftover seeds after she carved her pumpkin.

_____ 2. Working at the plant all day caused Gage to work up an appetite.

_____ 3. The plant was dying because it hadn't been watered for a week.

Challenge: Choose a definition, and write a sentence using the word *plant*.

_____

_____

turn over a new <u>leaf</u>	**A.** leaf (noun): the outgrowth of a green stem from a plant or tree
	B. leaf (noun): a sheet of metal or wood that can be placed in and taken out of a table

_____ 4. The leaves are the prettiest in the fall when they change color.

_____ 5. We painted leaves in art class when we were studying parts of a plant.

_____ 6. Don was having company over, so he put an extra leaf in the table.

Challenge: Choose a definition, and write a sentence using the word *leaf*.

_____

_____

Name _____ Date _____

Plants and Growing—Wacky Writing

Directions: Read and answer each prompt.

1. Describe a bad habit you have that could lead you to *turn over a new leaf*.

   _____

   _____

2. Describe a goal you have that you will not *let the grass grow under your feet* to accomplish.

   _____

   _____

3. Describe something you don't want to do, but you could *bloom where you are planted* and do a good job.

   _____

   _____

4. Name something your parents didn't want you to do at first, so you had to *plant a seed* and keep talking to them about it until they finally let you.

   _____

   _____

5. List three things you could do to *sow seeds of kindness* with your friends.

   _____

   _____

   _____

 51625—Go Figure! Exploring Figurative Language

Plants and Growing—Say What? Extensions

Directions: Choose two activities to complete.

> » bloom where you are planted   » plant a seed
>
> » sow seeds of kindness   » turn over a new leaf
>
> » don't let the grass grow under your feet

🖼 Figurative and Literal

Choose one figure of speech. Using a sheet of paper folded in half, write "literal" and "figurative" at the top of each side. Under "literal," draw your interpretation of the literal meaning of the figure of speech. Under "figurative," draw your interpretation of the figurative meaning of the figure of speech. Write the figure of speech on the back of your paper.

🔫 Say It, Don't Spray It!

Work with a small group to write and tell a story that includes all five figures of speech. One person begins the story. Then, each person takes a turn adding an idea to the story. Continue the story until all figures of speech have been used and the story comes to an end.

✋ Memory Game

Using five index cards, write each figure of speech on a separate card. Turn the cards over one at a time, and explain the definition of each phrase to a partner.

sowing seeds of kindness

Figures of Speech

» clear the air   » breath of fresh air

» floating on air   » leave it up in the air

» out of the clear blue sky

Overview

Students will enjoy learning about air- and sky-related idioms through the activities in this section. For detailed instructions on how to implement the activities in this lesson, see pages 8–10.

Materials

> copies of *Air and Sky Around Us—Match That Figure!* (page 31)
> copies of *Air and Sky Around Us—Choose That Figure!* (page 32)
> copies of *Air and Sky Around Us—Meaningful Words* (page 33)
> copies of *Air and Sky Around Us—Wacky Writing* (page 34)
> copies of *Air and Sky Around Us—Say What? Extensions* (page 35)
> scissors and glue

Additional Figures of Speech

> pie in the sky
> the sky's the limit
> air your dirty laundry
> vanish/disappear into thin air
> walk around with your nose in the air

Answer Key

Match That Figure! (page 31)
1. something new that makes the situation more exciting or interesting
2. to talk openly about a problem with someone
3. undecided about a question or decision
4. to feel free and happy about something that happened
5. something that happens suddenly

Pictures will vary, but should show an understanding for each figure of speech.

Choose That Figure! (page 32)
1. out of the clear blue sky
2. floating on air
3. breath of fresh air
4. clear the air

Challenge: Students create meaningful sentences with the figure of speech *leave it up in the air.*

Meaningful Words (page 33)
1. C   2. A   3. B
Challenge: Check sentences to be sure contexts match the definitions chosen.
4. B   5. A   6. B
Challenge: Check sentences to be sure contexts match the definitions chosen.

Wacky Writing (page 34)
Students' responses should accurately answer each prompt and demonstrate understanding of the figurative phrase.

Say What? Extensions (page 35)
Check to see that students have completed two of the three activities.

Air and Sky Around Us—Match That Figure!

Directions: Cut apart the definition cards. Glue each definition next to the correct phrase. Then, draw a picture to represent each figurative phrase.

Phrases	Definitions	Pictures
1. a breath of fresh air		
2. clear the air		
3. leave it up in the air		
4. floating on air		
5. out of the clear, blue sky		

something that happens suddenly	undecided about a question or decision	to feel free and happy about something that happened	something new that makes the situation more exciting or interesting	to talk openly about a problem with someone

Air and Sky Around Us—Choose That Figure!

Directions: Write the correct figure of speech in each sentence.

> » clear the air   » breath of fresh air
>
> » floating on air   » leave it up in the air
>
> » out of the clear blue sky

1. Last Monday, _____

    _____ my mom decided to take us to the movies.

2. Kimi was _____

    _____ after she found out she won the contest.

3. Starting school was a _____

    _____ for the students who were missing their friends over the summer.

4. Jefferson made Clare feel bad, so Clare decided to _____

    _____ and talk to him about it.

Challenge: Write a sentence using the figure of speech not used above.

_____

_____

_____

_____

Air and Sky Around Us—Meaningful Words

Directions: For each sentence, write the letter of the correct definition. Then, create your own sentence using the selected word.

out of the <u>clear</u> blue sky	**A.** clear (adjective): transparent or without color
	B. clear (verb): to clean off or remove objects
	C. clear (adjective): easy to understand or hear

_____ 1. The tour guide gave clear directions to the tourists before the hike.

_____ 2. The man's windows were clean, clear, and easy to see through.

_____ 3. Jimmy cleared off the table to put out the place settings for dinner.

Challenge: Choose a definition, and write a sentence using the word *clear*.

_____

_____

| breath of <u>fresh</u> air | **A.** fresh (adjective): newly made |
| | **B.** fresh (adjective): food straight from where it was grown; not yet cooked, canned, or frozen |

_____ 4. We picked fresh vegetables from our garden to eat for dinner.

_____ 5. The fresh paw prints in the snow showed us where to find our dog.

_____ 6. Instead of having frozen corn on the cob for dinner, we went to the market and got fresh corn.

Challenge: Choose a definition, and write a sentence using the word *fresh*.

_____

_____

Air and Sky Around Us—Wacky Writing

Directions: Read and answer each prompt.

1. Name something fun you like to do *out of the clear blue sky* when you are bored on the weekend.

   _____

   _____

2. Describe an event or activity that makes you *float on air*.

   _____

   _____

   _____

3. Describe a situation that you would not want to *leave up in the air*.

   _____

   _____

4. List three things that would be *breaths of fresh air* to have in your home.

   _____

   _____

   _____

5. Describe a time you were upset and had to *clear the air* with a friend or family member.

   _____

   _____

Air and Sky Around Us—Say What? Extensions

Directions: Choose two activities to complete.

> » clear the air
> » floating on air
> » out of the clear blue sky
> » breath of fresh air
> » leave it up in the air

📝 Poetry Time

Choose one figure of speech. Then, create a short poem or rap with eight lines that would help someone younger than you understand the meaning of the figure of speech. You can use the definition, examples, and your own creativity to make it fun and interesting.

✗✓ Example and Non-Example

Choose one figure of speech. Then, write two sentences using the figure of speech appropriately, and two using the figure of speech incorrectly. Read the four sentences to a partner, and have him or her figure out which two sentences are good examples and which two sentences are non-examples.

🎈 Floating on Air

Draw a picture of yourself sitting on a cloud. Then, write eight things on the page that make you really happy, or feel like you're *floating on air*.

floating on air

Figures of Speech

» drive someone to the edge   » ride the wave

» get someone's motor running » lose your train of thought

» throw someone under the bus

Overview

Students will enjoy learning about transportation-related idioms through the activities in this section. For detailed instructions on how to implement the activities in this lesson, see pages 8–10.

Materials

› copies of *Transportation—Match That Figure!* (page 37)

› copies of *Transportation—Choose That Figure!* (page 38)

› copies of *Transportation—Meaningful Words* (page 39)

› copies of *Transportation—Wacky Writing* (page 40)

› copies of *Transportation—Say What? Extensions* (page 41)

› scissors and glue

Additional Figures of Speech

> joyride

> bumpy ride

> in the fast lane

> hit a speed bump

> let something ride

> take someone for a ride

> hitch your wagon to a star

Answer Key

Match That Figure! (page 37)

1. to forget what you were thinking about
2. to blame someone else for something to save yourself
3. to make someone crazy by your actions
4. to get someone really excited about something
5. to be involved with activities that other people are already doing

Pictures will vary, but should show an understanding for each figure of speech.

Choose That Figure! (page 38)

1. lost his train of thought
2. drove her mom to the edge
3. got his motor running
4. threw his friend under the bus

Challenge: Students create meaningful sentences with the figure of speech *ride the wave.*

Meaningful Words (page 39)

1. A   2. B   3. C

Challenge: Check sentences to be sure contexts match the definitions chosen.

4. B   5. A   6. A

Challenge: Check sentences to be sure contexts match the definitions chosen.

Wacky Writing (page 40)

Students' responses should accurately answer each prompt and demonstrate understanding of the figurative phrase.

Say What? Extensions (page 41)

Check to see that students have completed two of the three activities.

Transportation—Match That Figure!

Directions: Cut apart the definition cards. Glue each definition next to the correct phrase. Then, draw a picture to represent each figurative phrase

Phrases	Definitions	Pictures
1. lose your train of thought		
2. throw someone under the bus		
3. drive to the edge		
4. get someone's motor running		
5. ride the wave		

to get someone really excited about something	to be involved with activities that other people are already doing	to blame someone else for something to save yourself	to forget what you were thinking about	to make someone crazy by your actions

Transportation—Choose That Figure!

Directions: Write the correct figure of speech in each sentence.

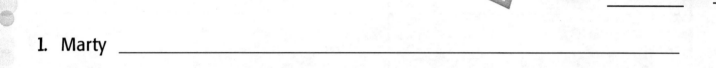

» drove her mom to the edge   » ride the wave

» got his motor running   » lost his train of thought

» threw his friend under the bus

1. Marty _____

   _____ when he heard the airplane fly by.

2. Jennifer _____

   _____ when she played the drums all night.

3. It really _____

   _____ when Todd found out he was chosen for the science team.

4. Not wanting to get in trouble himself, Graham _____

   _____ .

Challenge: Write a sentence using the figure of speech not used above.

_____

_____

_____

_____

Transportation—Meaningful Words

Directions: For each sentence, write the letter of the correct definition. Then, create your own sentence using the selected word.

lose your <u>train</u> of thought	A. train (noun): a connected group of rolling carts on a railroad track
	B. train (noun): a connected group of people or animals traveling together
	C. train (verb): to teach how to develop a skill or habit

_____ 1. The train left on time to get the travelers to work.

_____ 2. The ducklings formed a train as they walked toward the pond.

_____ 3. Mr. Killian had to train his children how to mow the lawn so they could do it themselves when he was out of town.

Challenge: Choose a definition, and write a sentence using the word *train*.

_____

_____

| <u>drive</u> to the edge | A. drive (verb): to cause to move forward with some force or motor |
| | B. drive (noun): an event designed by people working together for a cause |

_____ 4. The food drive provided thousands of cans of food for the homeless shelter.

_____ 5. Mika had to drive her daughter's team to their final basketball game.

_____ 6. Driving around the city during the holidays was a beautiful sight.

Challenge: Choose a definition, and write a sentence using the word *drive*.

_____

_____

Transportation—Wacky Writing

Directions: Read and answer each prompt.

1. List three pet peeves that might *drive you to the edge.*

   _____

   _____

2. Explain why it isn't a good idea to *throw a good friend under the bus.*

   _____

   _____

   _____

3. Describe something that would really *get your motor running.*

   _____

   _____

4. Name an action someone else might do that would cause you to *lose your train of thought.*

   _____

   _____

   _____

5. Explain why sometimes it's a good idea to *ride the wave* instead of doing your own thing.

   _____

   _____

Transportation—Say What? Extensions

Directions: Choose two activities to complete.

> » drive someone to the edge
> » get someone's motor running
> » throw someone under the bus
> » ride the wave
> » lose your train of thought

 ### Sing Me a Song

With a partner, write a simple song to a familiar tune. Include at least one of the figures of speech in your song. Share your song by singing it or reading the lyrics aloud like a poem.

 ### Short Story

Write a short description about something that recently happened to you using two of the figures of speech. Be sure the figures of speech are used correctly. Underline them when you are finished.

 ### Drive Me Crazy!

With a partner, think of five things that drive you crazy, or *drive you to the edge*. Keep listing things until you come up with five that you both agree on.

ride the wave

Figures of Speech

» live in the past

» go down in history

» history repeats itself

» the rest is history

» blast from the past

Overview

Students will enjoy learning about history-related idioms through the activities in this section. For detailed instructions on how to implement the activities in this lesson, see pages 8–10.

Materials

> copies of *History—Match That Figure!* (page 43)
> copies of *History—Choose That Figure!* (page 44)
> copies of *History—Meaningful Words* (page 45)
> copies of *History—Wacky Writing* (page 46)
> copies of *History—Say What? Extensions* (page 47)
> scissors and glue

Additional Figures of Speech

> past your prime
> a thing of the past
> that's ancient history
> you can't put that past me

Answer Key

Match That Figure! (page 43)

1. something good that reminds you of the past, often a surprise
2. everyone already knows what happened next
3. the same things seem to happen over and over
4. to focus more on what happened in the past than the present
5. to be recorded for history as an important person or event

Pictures will vary, but should show an understanding for each figure of speech.

Choose That Figure! (page 44)

1. go down in history
2. the rest was history
3. history repeated itself
4. blast from the past

Challenge: Students create meaningful sentences with the figure of speech *live in the past.*

Meaningful Words (page 45)

1. A   2. B   3. A

Challenge: Check sentences to be sure contexts match the definitions chosen.

4. B   5. B   6. A

Challenge: Check sentences to be sure contexts match the definitions chosen.

Wacky Writing (page 46)

Students' responses should accurately answer each prompt and demonstrate understanding of the figurative phrase.

Say What? Extensions (page 47)

Check to see that students have completed two of the three activities.

History—Match That Figure!

Directions: Cut apart the definition cards. Glue each definition next to the correct phrase. Then, draw a picture to represent each figurative phrase.

Phrases	Definitions	Pictures
1. blast from the past		
2. the rest is history		
3. history repeats itself		
4. live in the past		
5. go down in history		

the same things seem to happen over and over	to be recorded for history as an important person or event	to focus more on what happened in the past than the present	everyone already knows what happened next	something good that reminds you of the past, often a surprise

History—Choose That Figure!

Directions: Write the correct figure of speech in each sentence.

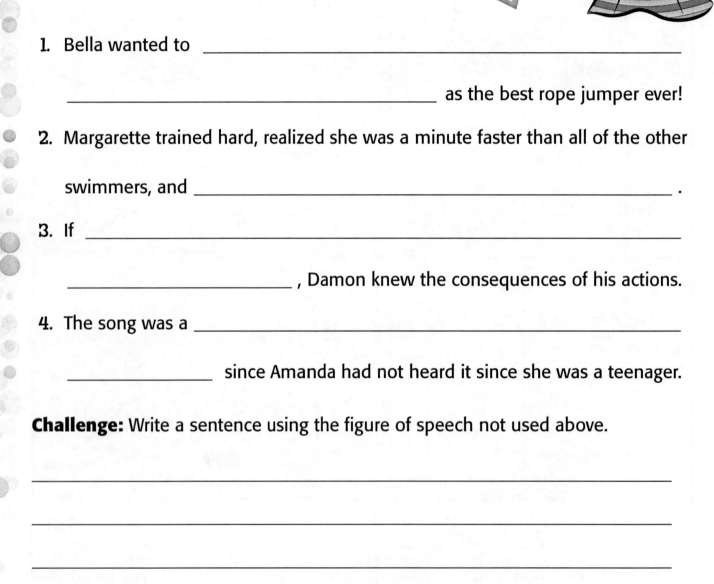

» live in the past   » go down in history

» blast from the past   » the rest was history

» history repeated itself

1. Bella wanted to _____

_____ as the best rope jumper ever!

2. Margarette trained hard, realized she was a minute faster than all of the other

swimmers, and _____ .

3. If _____

_____ , Damon knew the consequences of his actions.

4. The song was a _____

_____ since Amanda had not heard it since she was a teenager.

Challenge: Write a sentence using the figure of speech not used above.

_____

_____

_____

_____

History—Meaningful Words

Directions: For each sentence, write the letter of the correct definition. Then, create your own sentence using the selectwed word.

| blast from the past | A. past (noun): any time before the present that has gone by |
| | B. past (adjective): just beyond something |

____ 1. Thinking about the past when her puppy was little made Mia happy.

____ 2. My house is just past the stop sign on the left.

____ 3. Henry thought about all the fun he had in the past whenever he saw his grandfather.

Challenge: Choose a definition, and write a sentence using the word *past*.

_____

_____

| the rest is history | A. rest (noun): a time for sleeping or not being active |
| | B. rest (noun): the part that is left over |

____ 4. Janice didn't feel well, but the rest of the family went to the movies.

____ 5. Ennis put the rest of the pizza in the refrigerator after he finished eating.

____ 6. Liam needed a rest after working on the farm all day.

Challenge: Choose a definition, and write a sentence using the word *rest*.

_____

_____

History—Wacky Writing

Directions: Read and answer each prompt.

1. Explain one thing you know your parents will do over and over because *history repeats itself.*

   _____

   _____

2. Explain a moment when someone might say you were *living in the past.*

   _____

   _____

3. Describe one thing for which you would like to *go down in history.*

   _____

   _____

   _____

4. Explain one memory everyone in your family knows so well that when someone starts to tell it, you could say, *"the rest is history."*

   _____

   _____

   _____

5. Name three people who would be *blasts from your past* if they showed up at your door today.

   _____

   _____

51625—Go Figure! Exploring Figurative Language   © *Shell Education*

History—Say What? Extensions

Directions: Choose two activities to complete.

> » live in the past
>
> » blast from the past
>
> » history repeats itself
>
> » go down in history
>
> » the rest is history

 Sing Me a Song

With a partner, write a simple song to a familiar tune. Include at least one of the figures of speech in your song. Share your song by singing it or reading the lyrics aloud like a poem.

 Critical Thinking

Create a piece of artwork with symbols and pictures that represent the meaning of one of the figures of speech. You may not use any words in the piece. Share your picture with a partner or group to see if they can guess which figure of speech you chose.

👓 Read All About It!

With a partner, pretend you work for a news organization and have to write one paragraph about something that happened in your town. The story should contain at least two of this week's figures of speech.

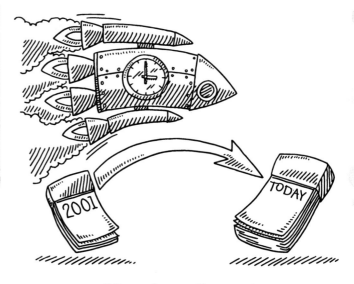

blast from the past

Figures of Speech

» make a living

» runs in the family

» bring down the house

» somewhere in the neighborhood

» eat them out of house and home

Overview

Students will enjoy learning about home- and community-related idioms through the activities in this section. For detailed instructions on how to implement the activities in this lesson, see pages 8–10.

Materials

> copies of *Homes and Communities—Match That Figure!* (page 49)

> copies of *Homes and Communities—Choose That Figure!* (page 50)

> copies of *Homes and Communities—Meaningful Words* (page 51)

> copies of *Homes and Communities—Wacky Writing* (page 52)

> copies of *Homes and Communities—Say What? Extensions* (page 53)

> scissors and glue

Additional Figures of Speech

> on the house

> not a living soul

> my house is your house

> living on borrowed time

> home is where the heart is

> wasn't a dry eye in the house

Answer Key

Match That Figure! (page 49)

1. an approximate amount or measurement of something

2. a quality or characteristic that appears in all members of a family

3. an exaggeration meaning to eat a large amount of food that has to keep being replaced

4. to put on a performance that the audience really loves

5. the way you make money to provide for yourself or your family

Pictures will vary, but should show an understanding for each figure of speech.

Choose That Figure! (page 50)

1. makes a living

2. somewhere in the neighborhood

3. eating them out of house and home

4. brought down the house

Challenge: Students create meaningful sentences with the figure of speech *runs in the family*.

Meaningful Words (page 51)

1. B   2. A   3. A

Challenge: Check sentences to be sure contexts match the definitions chosen.

4. B   5. A   6. B

Challenge: Check sentences to be sure contexts match the definitions chosen.

Wacky Writing (page 52)

Students' responses should accurately answer each prompt and demonstrate understanding of the figurative phrase.

Say What? Extensions (page 53)

Check to see that students have completed two of the three activities.

Homes and Communities—Match That Figure!

Directions: Cut apart the definition cards. Glue each definition next to the correct phrase. Then, draw a picture to represent each figurative phrase.

Phrases	Definitions	Pictures
1. somewhere in the neighborhood		
2. runs in the family		
3. eat them out of house and home		
4. bring down the house		
5. make a living		

an exaggeration meaning to eat a large amount of food that has to keep being replaced	an approximate amount or measurement of something	the way you make money to provide for yourself or your family	to put on a performance that the audience really loves	a quality or characteristic that appears in all members of a family

Homes and Communities—Choose That Figure!

Directions: Write the correct figure of speech in each sentence.

> » makes a living   » somewhere in the neighborhood
>
> » runs in the family   » brought down the house
>
> » eating them out of house and home

1. Cara's mother _____

   _____ as a lawyer.

2. The new video game cost _____

   _____ of $20.

3. Luke's parents complained he was _____

   _____ after every football practice.

4. Keenan _____

   _____ after he performed his dance at the talent show.

Challenge: Write a sentence using the figure of speech not used above.

_____

_____

_____

Homes and Communities—Meaningful Words

Directions: For each sentence, write the letter of the correct definition. Then, create your own sentence using the selected word.

| bring <u>down</u> the house | A. down (adverb): from higher to lower |
| | B. down (adjective): feeling sad or depressed |

_____ 1. Asher felt down after finding out the party was canceled.

_____ 2. Charlotte couldn't remember where she set her keys down at home.

_____ 3. Mario fell down after tripping over his shoelaces during the race.

Challenge: Choose a definition, and write a sentence using the word *down*.

_____

_____

| eat them out of house and <u>home</u> | A. home (noun): a place where people live |
| | B. home (adjective): the center of operations for a business or team |

_____ 4. The business's home office was located in Florida.

_____ 5. I ran home after school to tell my mom I won the spelling bee.

_____ 6. The baseball players were excited to be able to play a home game.

Challenge: Choose a definition, and write a sentence using the word *home*.

_____

_____

Homes and Communities—Wacky Writing

Directions: Read and answer each prompt.

1. Explain what you want to do to *make a living* when you get older.

   _____

   _____

   _____

2. Name three things that cost *somewhere in the neighborhood* of five dollars.

   _____

   _____

3. Describe something you could perform that would *bring down the house.*

   _____

   _____

   _____

4. Name three things that you love to eat that would make you *eat your parents out of house and home.*

   _____

   _____

   _____

5. List five character or physical traits *that run in your family.*

   _____

   _____

51625—Go Figure! Exploring Figurative Language   © Shell Education

Homes and Communities—Say What? Extensions

Directions: Choose two activities to complete.

> » somewhere in the neighborhood » runs in the family
>
> » bring down the house » make a living
>
> » eat them out of house and home

Figurative and Literal

Choose one figure of speech. Using a sheet of paper folded in half, write "literal" and "figurative" at the top of each side. Under "literal," draw your interpretation of the literal meaning of the figure of speech. Under "figurative," draw your interpretation of the figurative meaning of the figure of speech. Write the figure of speech on the back of your paper.

Short Story

Write a short description about something that recently happened to you using two of the figures of speech. Be sure the figures of speech are used correctly. Underline them when you are finished.

runs in the family

Mime Time

Take turns with your partner or group members acting out all five of the figures of speech. You may only use body language and gestures to act out the clues. You may not use your voice!

Figures of Speech

» state of mind   » state of the art

» out on the town   » paint the town red

» you can't fight city hall

Overview

Students will enjoy learning about city-, state-, and country-related idioms through the activities in this section. For detailed instructions on how to implement the activities in this lesson, see pages 8–10.

Materials

> copies of *Cities, States, and Countries—Match That Figure!* (page 55)

> copies of *Cities, States, and Countries—Choose That Figure!* (page 56)

> copies of *Cities, States, and Countries—Meaningful Words* (page 57)

> copies of *Cities, States, and Countries—Wacky Writing* (page 58)

> copies of *Cities, States, and Countries—Say What? Extensions* (page 59)

> scissors and glue

> index cards

Additional Figures of Speech

> city slicker

> get out of town!

> sad state of affairs

> American as apple pie

> talk of the town

Answer Key

Match That Figure! (page 55)

1. going out of the house for entertainment
2. something that is very current or up to date
3. your attitude toward a topic
4. it's hard to win a battle against people in charge
5. to go out to celebrate and have fun

Pictures will vary, but should show an understanding for each figure of speech.

Choose That Figure! (page 56)

1. out on the town
2. you can't fight city hall
3. state of the art
4. state of mind

Challenge: Students create meaningful sentences with the figure of speech *paint the town red*.

Meaningful Words (page 57)

1. B   2. A   3. B

Challenge: Check sentences to be sure contexts match the definitions chosen.

4. B   5. C   6. A

Challenge: Check sentences to be sure contexts match the definitions chosen.

Wacky Writing (page 58)

Students' responses should accurately answer each prompt and demonstrate understanding of the figurative phrase.

Say What? Extensions (page 59)

Check to see that students have completed two of the three activities.

Cities, States, and Countries—Match That Figure!

Directions: Cut apart the definition cards. Glue each definition next to the correct phrase. Then, draw a picture to represent each figurative phrase.

Phrases	Definitions	Pictures
1. out on the town		
2. state of the art		
3. state of mind		
4. you can't fight city hall		
5. paint the town red		

something that is very current or up to date.	it's hard to win a battle against people in charge	going out of the house for entertainment	your attitude toward a topic	to go out to celebrate and have fun

Cities, States, and Countries—Choose That Figure!

Directions: Write the correct figure of speech in each sentence.

> » state of mind   » state of the art
>
> » out on the town   » paint the town red
>
> » you can't fight city hall

1. Serena and her friends always went _____

   _____ on Friday nights.

2. Even though people said, " _____

   _____ ," the protestors still showed up to prove them wrong.

3. Because they received grant money for cutting-edge research, the hospital was

   _____ .

4. Being sad is a _____

   _____ , and it helps to focus on the positive.

Challenge: Write a sentence using the figure of speech not used above.

_____

_____

_____

_____

Cities, States, and Countries—Meaningful Words

Directions: For each sentence, write the letter of the correct definition. Then, create your own sentence using the selected word.

state of the art	**A.** state (noun): the condition of a person or thing
	B. state (noun): a unified area of a country such as the United States.

_____ 1. Ezra's dad had to move out of state because his job transferred him.

_____ 2. Amelia was in a state of shock when she found out she was going on vacation.

_____ 3. Oregon is a state along the coast of the Pacific Ocean.

Challenge: Choose a definition, and write a sentence using the word *state*.

_____

_____

state of **mind**	**A.** mind (noun): the part of the body where thinking and feeling takes place
	B. mind (verb): to obey or pay attention to
	C. mind (verb): to be bothered by

_____ 4. Wyatt was told to mind his manners at the dinner table.

_____ 5. I don't ever mind helping my friends when they are in need.

_____ 6. My heart told me to do one thing, but my mind told me to do another.

Challenge: Choose a definition, and write a sentence using the word *mind*.

_____

_____

Cities, States, and Countries—Wacky Writing

Directions: Read and answer each prompt.

1. Name three fun things you could do this weekend to *paint the town red*.

    _____

    _____

2. Although people say *you can't fight city hall*, describe how to best negotiate with your parents when you want to make a change at home.

    _____

    _____

3. Describe your *state of mind* before taking an important test.

    _____

    _____

    _____

4. Name who you would want to *go out on the town* with and why.

    _____

    _____

    _____

5. Describe something in your school that you think is *state of the art*.

    _____

    _____

© Shell Education

Cities, States, and Countries—Say What? Extensions

Directions: Choose two activities to complete.

> » state of mind   » state of the art
>
> » out on the town   » paint the town red
>
> » you can't fight city hall

 ### Say It, Don't Spray It!

Work with a group to write and tell a story that includes all five figures of speech. One person begins the story. Then, each person takes a turn adding an idea to the story. Continue the story until all figures of speech have been used and the story comes to an end.

✍ Poetry Time

Choose one of the figures of speech. Then, create a short poem or rap with eight lines that would help someone younger than you understand the meaning of the figure of speech. You can use the definition, examples, and your own creativity to make it fun and interesting.

 ### Memory Game

Using five index cards, write each figure of speech on a separate card. Turn the cards over one at a time, and explain the definition of each phrase to a partner.

paint the town red

Figures of Speech

» being raised in a barn

» cream of the crop

» good seed makes a good crop

» bet the farm

» couldn't hit the side of a barn

Overview

Students will enjoy learning about farming-related idioms through the activities in this section. For detailed instructions on how to implement the activities in this lesson, see pages 8–10.

Materials

> copies of *Farming—Match That Figure!* (page 61)
> copies of *Farming—Choose That Figure!* (page 62)
> copies of *Farming—Meaningful Words* (page 63)
> copies of *Farming—Wacky Writing* (page 64)
> copies of *Farming—Say What? Extensions* (page 65)
> scissors and glue
> index cards

Additional Figures of Speech

> pig sty
> crop out
> funny farm
> bought the farm
> farm something out
> can't make a silk purse out of a sow's ear

Answer Key

Match That Figure! (page 61)

1. spend all your money or resources in order to make more money in the end
2. the best person or thing
3. having poor manners
4. making something out of good material so the final product is much better
5. not having good aim or not being able to hit an easy target

Pictures will vary, but should show an understanding for each figure of speech.

Choose That Figure! (page 62)

1. couldn't hit the side of a barn
2. bet the farm
3. good seed makes a good crop
4. raised in a barn

Challenge: Students create meaningful sentences with the figure of speech *cream of the crop.*

Meaningful Words (page 63)

1. A 2. B 3. B

Challenge: Check sentences to be sure contexts match the definitions chosen.

4. B 5. A 6. A

Challenge: Check sentences to be sure contexts match the definitions chosen.

Wacky Writing (page 64)

Students' responses should accurately answer each prompt and demonstrate understanding of the figurative phrase.

Say What? Extensions (page 65)

Check to see that students have completed two of the three activities.

Name _____ Date _____

Farming—Match That Figure!

Directions: Cut apart the definition cards. Glue each definition next to the correct phrase. Then, draw a picture to represent each figurative phrase.

Phrases	Definitions	Pictures
1. bet the farm		
2. cream of the crop		
3. being raised in a barn		
4. good seed makes a good crop		
5. couldn't hit the side of a barn		

spend all your money or resources in order to make more money in the end	not having good aim or not being able to hit an easy target	making something out of good material so the final product is much better	the best person or thing	having poor manners

Farming—Choose That Figure!

Directions: Write the correct figure of speech in each sentence.

> » raised in a barn
> » cream of the crop
> » good seed makes a good crop
> » bet the farm
> » couldn't hit the side of a barn

1. Without his glasses, Bradley _____

   _____ while playing dodge ball.

2. Laurie _____

   _____ and invested all her money to buy a food truck.

3. Ashley's parents wanted to pay extra for leather seats in their car because

   _____ ,

   and they knew the car would last longer with better material.

4. "You act like you were _____

   with bad manners like that!" Mom yelled to the kids at the dinner table.

Challenge: Write a sentence using the figure of speech not used above.

_____

_____

_____

_____

Farming—Meaningful Words

Directions: For each sentence, write the letter of the correct definition. Then, create your own sentence using the selected word.

| cream of the crop | A. crop (noun): the bundle of things grown on farmland |
| | B. crop (verb): to reduce the size of something by cutting down edges or parts |

_____ 1. Due to the bad weather, the crops this year didn't produce as much product as last season.

_____ 2. Liam cropped the photograph so that he was the only one in it.

_____ 3. I had to crop the tablecloths so they would fit the tables for the wedding.

Challenge: Choose a definition, and write a sentence using the word *crop*.

_____

_____

| good seed makes a good crop | A. seed (noun): the small, fertilized part of a plant used for regrowth |
| | B. seed (verb): to sow or scatter a field for future growth |

_____ 4. The farmer seeded the land to get ready for the next season.

_____ 5. Heidi pulled out the seeds before eating the watermelon.

_____ 6. We planted the seeds and measured the bean plant every day.

Challenge: Choose a definition, and write a sentence using the word *seed*.

_____

_____

Farming—Wacky Writing

Directions: Read and answer each prompt.

1. Describe an activity in which a person *couldn't hit the side of a barn*.

   _____

   _____

2. Name three things you might do that would make someone think you were *raised in a barn*.

   _____

   _____

3. Since *good seed makes good crop*, explain something you would make that would be worth using more expensive materials.

   _____

   _____

4. Describe a *cream of the crop* item you would like for your next birthday.

   _____

   _____

   _____

5. Describe one thing you would *bet the farm* on. Explain why.

   _____

   _____

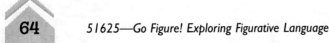

Farming—Say What? Extensions

Directions: Choose two activities to complete.

> » raised in a barn　　　» cream of the crop
>
> » good seed makes good crop　» bet the farm
>
> » couldn't hit the side of a barn

✗✓ Example and Non-Example

Choose one figure of speech. Then, write two sentences using the figure of speech appropriately, and two using the figure of speech incorrectly. Read the four sentences to a partner, and have him or her figure out which two sentences are good examples and which two sentences are non-examples.

◀▶ Matching Game

Create a matching game with a partner. Using 10 index cards, write each figure of speech on one card and your own definition for each phrase on another card. Mix up all the cards. Time how long it takes you to match each figure of speech with its definition. Have your partner try to beat your time. Each person goes twice to see who can achieve the fastest time.

Tell Me a Tale

Create a fairy tale with a small group. The story should be funny, short, and use at least two figures of speech. Each person can only say one word at a time to tell the story. For example, the first person might say "once." Then, the next person would say "upon." The third person would say "a," and the fourth person would say "time."

couldn't hit the side of a barn

Law and Justice

Figures of Speech

» judge not, lest you be judged

» take the law into your own hands

» on the wrong side of the law

» you can't judge a book by its cover

» have the ball in one's court

Overview

Students will enjoy learning about law- and justice-related idioms through the activities in this section. For detailed instructions on how to implement the activities in this lesson, see pages 8–10.

Materials

> copies of *Law and Justice—Match That Figure!* (page 67)

> copies of *Law and Justice—Choose That Figure!* (page 68)

> copies of *Law and Justice—Meaningful Words* (page 69)

> copies of *Law and Justice—Wacky Writing* (page 70)

> copies of *Law and Justice—Say What? Extensions* (page 71)

> scissors and glue

Additional Figures of Speech

> do justice

> her word is law

> long arm of the law

> throw the book at someone

> judge someone on his/her own merits

Answer Key

Match That Figure! (page 67)

1. to punish someone yourself instead of reporting them
2. outward appearances can't tell you what someone is really like
3. being responsible for the next move or decision
4. doing something illegal
5. no one is perfect, so don't criticize the behavior of others

Pictures will vary, but should show an understanding for each figure of speech.

Choose That Figure! (page 68)

1. on the wrong side of the law
2. took the law into her own hands
3. judge a book by its cover
4. the ball was in my court

Challenge: Students create meaningful sentences with the figure of speech *judge not, lest you be judged*.

Meaningful Words (page 69)

1. B   2. B   3. A

Challenge: Check sentences to be sure contexts match the definitions chosen.

4. B   5. A   6. A

Challenge: Check sentences to be sure contexts match the definitions chosen.

Wacky Writing (page 70)

Students' responses should accurately answer each prompt and demonstrate understanding of the figurative phrase.

Say What? Extensions (page 71)

Check to see that students have completed two of the three activities.

Law and Justice—Match That Figure!

Directions: Cut apart the definition cards. Glue each definition next to the correct phrase. Then, draw a picture to represent each figurative phrase.

Phrases	Definitions	Pictures
1. take the law into your own hands		
2. you can't judge a book by its cover		
3. have the ball in one's court		
4. on the wrong side of the law		
5. judge not, lest you be judged		

being responsible for the next move or decision	no one is perfect, so don't criticize the behavior of others	outward appearances can't tell you what someone is really like	to punish someone yourself instead of reporting them	doing something illegal

Name _____ Date _____

Law and Justice—Choose That Figure!

Directions: Write the correct figure of speech in each sentence.

» judge not, lest you be judged   » on the wrong side of the law

» judge a book by its cover   » the ball was in my court

» took the law into her own hands

1. When Billy got in trouble at school, he knew he was _____

   _____ .

2. When they had a dispute, Lea _____

   _____ to solve the conflict instead of telling an adult.

3. My mom told me never to _____

   _____, so I tried to get to know all my classmates.

4. I knew that _____

   when the group was split, and I was the only one left to vote.

Challenge: Write a sentence using the figure of speech not used above.

_____

_____

_____

_____

Law and Justice—Meaningful Words

Directions: For each sentence, write the letter of the correct definition. Then, create your own sentence using the selected word.

have the ball in one's <u>court</u>	**A.** court (noun): a place where justice and law is administered **B.** court (noun): an open area or sports arena

____ 1. After the basketball game, many of the spectators ran onto the court.

____ 2. The open court at the park was full of birds.

____ 3. People have to go to court if they break the law.

Challenge: Choose a definition, and write a sentence using the word *court.*

_____

_____

you can't judge a <u>book</u> by its cover	**A.** book (noun): sheets of paper bound together with writing on them **B.** book (verb): to make a reservation or register for something

____ 4. We booked a table at the restaurant for eight o'clock.

____ 5. The author wrote a personal note in the book for the little boy.

____ 6. Amelia gave the book to José when she was done reading it.

Challenge: Choose a definition, and write a sentence using the word *book.*

_____

_____

Law and Justice—Wacky Writing

Directions: Read and answer each prompt.

1. Describe why *judge not, lest you be judged* is a good rule to follow in life.

   _____

   _____

2. Explain why you would not want to be *on the wrong side of the law.*

   _____

   _____

3. Describe a situation in which a person should *take the law into his or her hands.*

   _____

   _____

   _____

4. Tell about a time that you *judged a book by its cover* and were wrong.

   _____

   _____

   _____

5. Describe a time when you were glad you *had the ball in your court.*

   _____

   _____

   _____

Law and Justice—Say What? Extensions

Directions: Choose two activities to complete.

> » judge not, lest you be judged
>
> » take the law into your own hands
>
> » you can't judge a book by its cover
>
> » have the ball in one's court
>
> » on the wrong side of the law

Comic Strip

Create a short four- to six-frame comic strip with sketches or simple pictures. Show the humor of one character using a figure of speech and the other character taking it literally.

☆ Wrong Side of the Law

With a partner, think about an important historical figure that "took the law into his or her own hands." Explain what happened. What was the outcome of this action?

I'm the Judge

Work with a partner. Share a time when you met someone and *judged a book by its cover* but realized he or she was different once you got to know him or her.

have the ball in one's court

Figures of Speech

» bear hug

» smarter than the average bear

» hungry as a bear

» like bears to honey

» claw your way out of something

Overview

Students will enjoy learning about bear-related idioms through the activities in this section. For detailed instructions on how to implement the activities in this lesson, see pages 8–10.

Materials

> copies of *Bears—Match That Figure!* (page 73)
> copies of *Bears—Choose That Figure!* (page 74)
> copies of *Bears—Meaningful Words* (page 75)
> copies of *Bears—Wacky Writing* (page 76)
> copies of *Bears—Say What? Extensions* (page 77)
> scissors and glue

Additional Figures of Speech

> bear down
> mama bear
> bear in mind
> gruff as a bear
> like a bear with a sore head

Answer Key

Match That Figure! (page 73)
1. a big hug
2. really hungry
3. to work hard to get yourself out of a difficult situation
4. easily attracting something
5. smarter than most people, a term from Yogi Bear®, a popular television cartoon for many years

Pictures will vary, but should show an understanding for each figure of speech.

Choose That Figure! (page 74)
1. bear hug
2. hungry as bears
3. like bears to honey
4. smarter than the average bear

Challenge: Students create meaningful sentences with the figure of speech *claw your way out of something*.

Meaningful Words (page 75)
1. A   2. B   3. B
Challenge: Check sentences to be sure contexts match the definitions chosen.
4. A   5. B   6. B
Challenge: Check sentences to be sure contexts match the definitions chosen.

Wacky Writing (page 76)
Students' responses should accurately answer each prompt and demonstrate understanding of the figurative phrase.

Say What? Extensions (page 77)
Check to see that students have completed two of the three activities.

Bears—Match That Figure!

Directions: Cut apart the definition cards. Glue each definition next to the correct phrase. Then, draw a picture to represent each figurative phrase.

Phrases	Definitions	Pictures
1. bear hug		
2. hungry as a bear		
3. claw your way out of something		
4. like bears to honey		
5. smarter than the average bear		

| really hungry | easily attracting something | a big hug | smarter than most people, a term from Yogi Bear®, a popular TV cartoon for many years. | to work hard to get yourself out of a difficult situation |

Bears—Choose That Figure!

Directions: Write the correct figure of speech in each sentence.

> » bear hug   » smarter than the average bear
>
> » hungry as bears   » like bears to honey
>
> » claw your way out of something

1. I was so excited to see my grandpa after four years that I ran up to him

   and gave him a _____ .

2. After soccer practice, we were all as _____

   _____ .

3. When Jung came to school with a big bag of snacks, the kids ran over to him

   _____ .

4. When Wanda solved the math problem first, she felt like she was _____

   _____ .

Challenge: Write a sentence using the figure of speech not used above.

_____

_____

_____

_____

Name _____   Date _____

Bears—Meaningful Words

Directions: For each sentence, write the letter of the correct definition. Then, create your own sentence using the selected word.

| <u>claw</u> one's way out of something | **A.** claw (noun): a sharp, usually curved nail on an animal |
| | **B.** claw (verb): to tear or scratch at with hands |

_____ 1. The cat's claws ruined Becca's new jacket.

_____ 2. The bear clawed his way through the bushes looking for his dinner.

_____ 3. The baby was clawing at the toys trying to reach them.

Challenge: Choose a definition, and write a sentence using the word *claw*.

_____

_____

| hungry as a <u>bear</u> | **A.** bear (noun): a mammal with a massive body and fur |
| | **B.** bear (verb): to hold up or support |

_____ 4. While camping, we were scared that bears were going to smell our food.

_____ 5. The blocks could not bear the weight anymore and collapsed.

_____ 6. I put the heavy boxes on my shoulders to help bear the weight.

Challenge: Choose a definition, and write a sentence using the word *bear*.

_____

_____

Name _____ Date _____

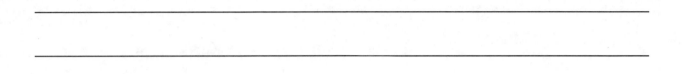

Bears—Wacky Writing

Directions: Read and answer each prompt.

1. What present might cause you to give someone a big *bear hug*? Why?

    _____

    _____

    _____

2. Describe a time you lied and had to *claw your way out* and tell the truth.

    _____

    _____

3. Name four things you love to eat when you are as *hungry as a bear*.

    _____

    _____

4. Explain one thing you like doing because you are *smarter than the average bear*.

    _____

    _____

    _____

5. What are three things that would make you run like *bears to honey* if you saw them in a store?

    _____

    _____

Name _____ Date _____

Bears—Say What? Extensions

Directions: Choose two activities to complete.

> » bear hug   » smarter than the average bear
>
> » hungry as bears   » like bears to honey
>
> » claw your way out of something

Read All About It!

With a partner, pretend you work for a news organization and have to write one paragraph about something that happened in your town. The story should contain at least two of this week's figures of speech.

Figurative and Literal

Choose one figure of speech. Using a sheet of paper folded in half, write "literal" and "figurative" at the top of each side. Under "literal," draw your interpretation of the literal meaning of the figure of speech. Under "figurative," draw your interpretation of the figurative meaning of the figure of speech. Write the figure of speech on the back of your paper.

♪ Sing Me a Song

With a partner, write a simple song to a familiar tune. Include at least one of the figures of speech in your song. Share your song by singing it or reading the lyrics aloud like a poem.

hungry as a bear

Figures of Speech

» birds of a feather flock together   » waiting in the wings

» the early bird catches the worm   » bird's-eye view

» a bird in the hand is worth two in the bush

Overview

Students will enjoy learning about bird-related idioms through the activities in this section. For detailed instructions on how to implement the activities in this lesson, see pages 8–10.

Materials

> copies of *Birds—Match That Figure!* (page 79)
> copies of *Birds—Choose That Figure!* (page 80)
> copies of *Birds—Meaningful Words* (page 81)
> copies of *Birds—Wacky Writing* (page 82)
> copies of *Birds—Say What? Extensions* (page 83)
> scissors and glue
> index cards

Additional Figures of Speech

> wing it
> bird brain
> a rare bird
> free as a bird
> a little birdy told me
> take under one's wing
> what's good for the goose is good for the gander

Answer Key

Match That Figure! (page 79)

1. people who are similar tend to hang out together
2. you will have success if you get a head start before everyone else
3. to get a broad view, where you can see the big parts, not just the details
4. ready to do something or substitute for someone as you are needed
5. having certainty is better than the possibility of something more or better later

Pictures will vary, but should show an understanding for each figure of speech.

Choose That Figure! (page 80)

1. the early bird catches the worm
2. birds of a feather flock together
3. waiting in the wings
4. bird's-eye view

Challenge: Students create meaningful sentences with the figure of speech *a bird in the hand is worth two in the bush*.

Meaningful Words (page 81)

1. A   2. B   3. A

Challenge: Check sentences to be sure contexts match the definitions chosen.
4. A   5. B   6. A

Challenge: Check sentences to be sure contexts match the definitions chosen.

Wacky Writing (page 82)

Students' responses should accurately answer each prompt and demonstrate understanding of the figurative phrase.

Say What? Extensions (page 83)

Check to see that students have completed two of the three activities.

Birds—Match That Figure!

Directions: Cut apart the definition cards. Glue each definition next to the correct phrase. Then, draw a picture to represent each figurative phrase.

Phrases	Definitions	Pictures
1. birds of a feather flock together		
2. the early bird catches the worm		
3. bird's-eye view		
4. waiting in the wings		
5. a bird in the hand is worth two in the bush		

to get a broad view, where you can see the big parts, not just the details	ready to do something or substitute for someone as you are needed	people who are similar tend to hang out together	you will have success if you get a head start before everyone else	having certainty is better than the possibility of something more or better later

51625—Go Figure! Exploring Figurative Language

Birds—Choose That Figure!

Directions: Write the correct figure of speech in each sentence.

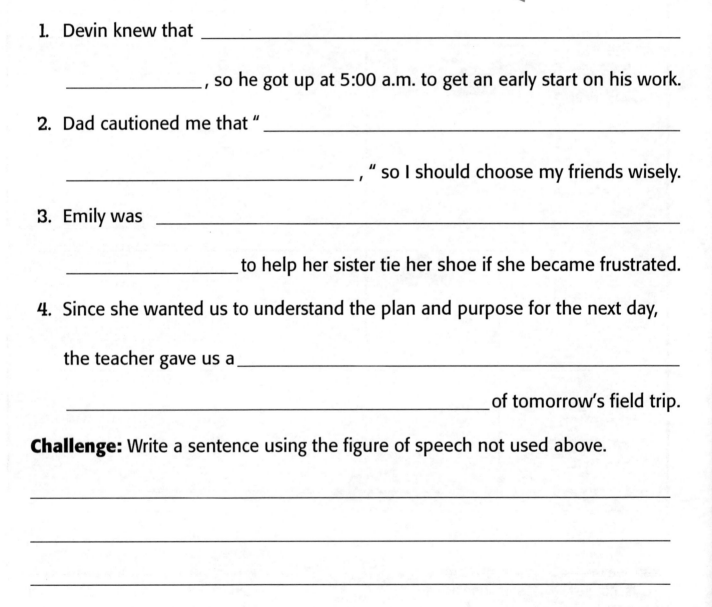

» birds of a feather flock together   » waiting in the wings

» the early bird catches the worm   » bird's-eye view

» a bird in the hand is worth two in the bush

1. Devin knew that _____

   _____ , so he got up at 5:00 a.m. to get an early start on his work.

2. Dad cautioned me that " _____

   _____ , " so I should choose my friends wisely.

3. Emily was _____

   _____ to help her sister tie her shoe if she became frustrated.

4. Since she wanted us to understand the plan and purpose for the next day,

   the teacher gave us a _____

   _____ of tomorrow's field trip.

Challenge: Write a sentence using the figure of speech not used above.

_____

_____

_____

Name _____ Date _____

Birds—Meaningful Words

Directions: For each sentence, write the letter of the correct definition. Then, create your own sentence using the selected word.

| birds of a feather flock together | A. flock (noun): a group of one kind of animal |
| | B. flock (verb): people or animals moving together to form a crowd |

_____ 1. The flock of geese was swimming in the lake.

_____ 2. The students flocked to their favorite teacher, Mrs. Rogers, in September.

_____ 3. The flock of people crowded around the store for the big sale.

Challenge: Choose a definition, and write a sentence using the word *flock*.

_____

_____

| bird's-eye view | A. view (noun): the range of a landscape or scene you can see |
| | B. view (noun): a person's opinion on a topic |

_____ 4. We had a beautiful view from our hotel room on our vacation.

_____ 5. My view on how much television to watch is different from my mom's.

_____ 6. Standing at the top of the mountain, I could see the view of the entire city.

Challenge: Choose a definition, and write a sentence using the word *view*.

_____

_____

Name _____ Date _____

Birds—Wacky Writing

Directions: Read and answer each prompt.

1. Since *the early bird catches the worm*, explain something that you think would be worth getting up early to do.

   _____

   _____

   _____

2. Explain why a *bird in the hand is worth two in the bush*.

   _____

   _____

3. Describe a time you were *waiting in the wings* to do something.

   _____

   _____

4. Describe a time when you had a clear *bird's-eye view* of what was going on around you.

   _____

   _____

5. Since *birds of a feather flock together*, describe what type of friends you usually hang out with.

   _____

   _____

   _____

51625—Go Figure! Exploring Figurative Language   © *Shell Education*

Name _____ Date _____

Birds—Say What? Extensions

Directions: Choose two activities to complete.

> » the early bird catches the worm » waiting in the wings
>
> » birds of a feather flock together » bird's-eye view
>
> » a bird in the hand is worth two in the bush

🔫 Say It, Don't Spray It!

Work with a group to write and tell a story that includes all five figures of speech. One person begins the story. Then, each person takes a turn adding an idea to the story. Continue the story until all figures of speech have been used and the story comes to an end.

◀▶ Matching Game

Create a matching game with a partner. Using 10 index cards, write each figure of speech on one card and your own definition for each phrase on another card. Mix up all the cards. Time how long it takes you to match each figure of speech with its definition. Have your partner try to beat your time. Each person goes twice to see who can achieve the fastest time.

▱ Comic Strip

Create a short four- to six-frame comic strip with sketches or simple pictures. Show the humor of one character using a figure of speech and the other character taking it literally.

the early bird catches the worm

51625—Go Figure! Exploring Figurative Language

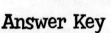

Figures of Speech

» curiosity killed the cat

» the cat got your tongue

» looks like something the cat dragged in

» copycat

» it's raining cats and dogs

Overview

Students will enjoy learning about cat-related idioms through the activities in this section. For detailed instructions on how to implement the activities in this lesson, see pages 8–10.

Materials

> copies of *Cats—Match That Figure!* (page 85)
> copies of *Cats—Choose That Figure!* (page 86)
> copies of *Cats—Meaningful Words* (page 87)
> copies of *Cats—Wacky Writing* (page 88)
> copies of *Cats—Say What? Extensions* (page 89)
> scissors and glue
> index cards

Additional Figures of Speech

> scaredy-cat
> the cat's meow
> play cat and mouse
> fight like cats and dogs
> the cat is out of the bag
> more than one way to skin a cat

Answer Key

Match That Figure! (page 85)

1. raining really hard
2. telling someone to speak when they are being quiet, but should be talking
3. being too curious about something can sometimes get you in trouble
4. being very untidy or dirty
5. someone that does the exact same thing as another person

Pictures will vary, but should show an understanding for each figure of speech.

Choose That Figure! (page 86)

1. copycat
2. it's raining cats and dogs
3. looked like something the cat dragged in
4. curiosity killed the cat

Challenge: Students create meaningful sentences with the figure of speech *the cat got your tongue*.

Meaningful Words (page 87)

1. A   2. B   3. A

Challenge: Check sentences to be sure contexts match the definitions chosen.

4. A   5. B   6. B

Challenge: Check sentences to be sure contexts match the definitions chosen.

Wacky Writing (page 88)

Students' responses should accurately answer each prompt and demonstrate understanding of the figurative phrase.

Say What? Extensions (page 89)

Check to see that students have completed two of the three activities.

Cats—Match That Figure!

Directions: Cut apart the definition cards. Glue each definition next to the correct phrase. Then, draw a picture to represent each figurative phrase.

Phrases	Definitions	Pictures
1. it's raining cats and dogs		
2. the cat got your tongue		
3. curiosity killed the cat		
4. looks like something the cat dragged in		
5. copycat		

telling a person to speak when they are quiet, but should be talking	being very untidy or dirty	someone that does the exact same thing as another person	being too curious about something can sometimes get you in trouble	raining really hard

Cats—Choose That Figure!

Directions: Write the correct figure of speech in each sentence.

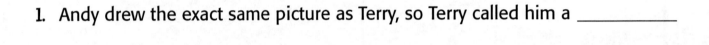

> » curiosity killed the cat   » copycat
>
> » the cat got your tongue   » it's raining cats and dogs
>
> » looked like something the cat dragged in

1. Andy drew the exact same picture as Terry, so Terry called him a _____

   _____ .

2. Dad announced, "_____

   _____ " after checking the weather from the window.

3. After playing outside in the mud for hours, the young child _____

   _____ .

4. Alek wanted to listen in on the adults' conversation, but his dad caught him

   and told him, "_____ !"

Challenge: Write a sentence using the figure of speech not used above.

_____

_____

_____

_____

Cats—Meaningful Words

Directions: For each sentence, write the letter of the correct definition. Then, create your own sentence using the selected word.

| copycat | A. copy (verb): to reproduce pictures or words, often with a machine |
| | B. copy (noun): the actual reproduction of an original document |

_____ 1. Mrs. Mars had to copy the worksheet for all of her students.

_____ 2. I found a copy of the book I needed for my book club.

_____ 3. Josiah missed class, so he had to copy the notes from a classmate.

Challenge: Choose a definition, and write a sentence using the word *copy*.

_____

_____

| its <u>raining</u> cats and dogs | A. rain (noun): water falling from clouds |
| | B. rain (verb): large amounts of things falling down |

_____ 4. We cancel school when the snow is heavy but not when the rain is heavy.

_____ 5. The tears rained from their eyes as they watched their son graduate from high school.

_____ 6. The ashes from the volcano rained down on the city.

Challenge: Choose a definition, and write a sentence using the word *raining*.

_____

_____

Cats—Wacky Writing

Directions: Read and answer each prompt.

1. Name three fun things to do when *it's raining cats and dogs*.

   _____

   _____

2. Since *curiosity killed the cat*, describe a time when you got in trouble for being nosy.

   _____

   _____

3. Describe a time when it's okay to be a *copycat*.

   _____

   _____

   _____

4. Tell about a time when the *cat got your tongue*, and you didn't know what to say.

   _____

   _____

   _____

5. Name something fun you have never done before that would make you *look like something the cat dragged in* when you were done.

   _____

   _____

51625—Go Figure! Exploring Figurative Language

Name _____ Date _____

Cats—Say What? Extensions

Directions: Choose two activities to complete.

> » curiosity killed the cat
> » the cat got your tongue
> » looks like something the cat dragged in
> » copycat
> » it's raining cats and dogs

 Short Story

Write a short description about something that recently happened to you using two of the figures of speech. Be sure the figures of speech are used correctly. Underline them when you are finished.

 Critical Thinking

Create a piece of artwork with symbols and pictures that represent the meaning of one of the figures of speech. You may not use any words in the piece. Share your picture with a partner or group to see if they can guess which figure of speech you chose.

 Memory Game

Using five index cards, write each figure of speech on a separate card. Turn the cards over one at a time, and explain the definition of each phrase to a partner.

it's raining cats and dogs

Figures of Speech

» straight from the horse's mouth

» hold your horses

» look a gift horse in the mouth

» eat like a horse

» you can lead a horse to water but you can't make him drink

Overview

Students will enjoy learning about horse-related idioms through the activities in this section. For detailed instructions on how to implement the activities in this lesson, see pages 8–10.

Materials

> copies of *Horses—Match That Figure!* (page 91)

> copies of *Horses—Choose That Figure!* (page 92)

> copies of *Horses—Meaningful Words* (page 93)

> copies of *Horses—Wacky Writing* (page 94)

> copies of *Horses—Say What? Extensions* (page 95)

> scissors and glue

Additional Figures of Speech

> dark horse

> charley-horse

> horsing around

> one-horse town

> climb on a high horse

> don't put the cart before the horse

> if wishes were horses, then beggars would ride

Answer Key

Match That Figure! (page 91)

1. to eat large amounts of food
2. telling someone to slow down
3. you can help or encourage, but you can't force someone to do something
4. being unthankful when given something
5. hearing information directly from a person, not second-hand

Pictures will vary, but should show an understanding for each figure of speech.

Choose That Figure! (page 92)

1. you can lead a horse to water, but you can't make him drink
2. look a gift horse in the mouth
3. straight from the horse's mouth
4. ate like a horse

Challenge: Students create meaningful sentences with the figure of speech *hold your horses*.

Meaningful Words (page 93)

1. A   2. B   3. B

Challenge: Check sentences to be sure contexts match the definitions chosen.

4. A   5. B   6. A

Challenge: Check sentences to be sure contexts match the definitions chosen.

Wacky Writing (page 94)

Students' responses should accurately answer each prompt and demonstrate understanding of the figurative phrase.

Say What? Extensions (page 95)

Check to see that students have completed two of the three activities.

Horses—Match That Figure!

Directions: Cut apart the definition cards. Glue each definition next to the correct phrase. Then, draw a picture to represent each figurative phrase.

Phrases	Definitions	Pictures
1. eat like a horse		
2. hold your horses		
3. you can lead a horse to water, but you can't make him drink		
4. look a gift horse in the mouth		
5. straight from the horse's mouth		

you can help or encourage, but you can't force someone to do something	to eat large amounts of food	being unthankful when given something	hearing information directly from a person, not second-hand	telling someone to slow down

Horses—Choose That Figure!

Directions: Write the correct figure of speech in each sentence.

> » straight from the horse's mouth » hold your horses
>
> » look a gift horse in the mouth » ate like a horse
>
> » you can lead a horse to water, but you can't make him drink

1. Kobe's mom tried to help him get his homework done, but he still didn't

   finish because _____

   _____ .

2. Danny wanted a new bike for his birthday, but he didn't complain when he

   got a skateboard because you shouldn't _____ .

3. I knew Mom got a new job because I heard the information _____

   _____ when she told me about it.

4. Mr. McDonald was so hungry after the race that he _____

   _____ .

Challenge: Write a sentence using the figure of speech not used above.

_____

_____

_____

_____

Horses—Meaningful Words

Directions: For each sentence, write the letter of the correct definition. Then, create your own sentence using the selected word.

hold your <u>horses</u>	**A.** horse (noun): a large, hoofed, four-footed animal used for riding or carrying items
	B. horse (verb): to mess around

_____ 1. I wonder which horse will win the Kentucky Derby this year?

_____ 2. Since the teacher was absent, the students horsed around a little.

_____ 3. My brother decided to horse around at church and got in trouble.

Challenge: Choose a definition, and write a sentence using the word *horses*.

_____

_____

look a <u>gift</u> horse in the mouth	**A.** gift (noun): something given to someone to honor or show caring
	B. gift (verb): to give someone a present

_____ 4. Molly got a ton of gifts at her baby shower.

_____ 5. As a group, we decided to gift the new teacher a coffee mug.

_____ 6. The best gift for birthdays is hanging out with your friends.

Challenge: Choose a definition, and write a sentence using the word *gift*.

_____

_____

Horses—Wacky Writing

Directions: Read and answer each prompt.

1. Describe why you wouldn't *look a gift horse in the mouth* if your grandma sent you five dollars.

   _____

   _____

2. Describe why the saying *you can lead a horse to water, but you can't make him drink* is true when you are trying to help a friend.

   _____

   _____

3. Name the top five things you would like to eat if you wanted to *eat like a horse*.

   _____

   _____

4. Explain what news you would have to hear *straight from the horse's mouth* to believe.

   _____

   _____

5. Describe a time when you were rushing to do something and someone told you to *hold your horses*.

   _____

   _____

Horses—Say What? Extensions

Directions: Choose two activities to complete.

> » straight from the horse's mouth   » hold your horses
>
> » look a gift horse in the mouth   » eat like a horse
>
> » you can lead a horse to water, but you can't make him drink

✗✓ Example and Non-Example

Choose one figure of speech. Then, write two sentences using the figure of speech appropriately, and two using the figure of speech incorrectly. Read the four sentences to a partner, and have him or her figure out which two sentences are good examples and which two sentences are non-examples.

Tell Me a Tale

Create a fairy tale with a small group. The story should be funny, short, and use at least two figures of speech. Each person can only say one word at a time to tell the story. For example, the first person might say "once." Then, the next person would say "upon." The third person would say "a," and the fourth person would say "time."

Mime Time

Take turns with your partner or group members acting out all five of the figures of speech. You may only use body language and gestures to act out the clues. You may not use your voice!

hold your horses

Figures of Speech

» still waters run deep

» big fish in a small pond

» swim with the sharks

» water under the bridge

» fishing for a compliment

Overview

Students will enjoy learning about sea-related idioms through the activities in this section. For detailed instructions on how to implement the activities in this lesson, see pages 8–10.

Materials

> copies of *Sea Life—Match That Figure!* (page 97)

> copies of *Sea Life—Choose That Figure!* (page 98)

> copies of *Sea Life—Meaningful Words* (page 99)

> copies of *Sea Life—Wacky Writing* (page 100)

> copies of *Sea Life—Say What? Extensions* (page 101)

> scissors and glue

Additional Figures of Speech

> sink or swim

> in deep water

> muddy the water

> have a whale of a time

> plenty of fish in the sea

> bridge over troubled waters

Answer Key

Match That Figure! (page 97)

1. someone who is important or successful only in a small group
2. something bad that happened in the past that cannot be changed
3. to be around or hang around bad or dangerous people
4. doing or saying something so that someone says something nice about you
5. quiet people are often careful thinkers

Pictures will vary, but should show an understanding for each figure of speech.

Choose That Figure! (page 98)

1. fishing for a compliment
2. water under the bridge
3. swim with the sharks
4. still waters run deep

Challenge: Students create meaningful sentences with the figure of speech *big fish in a small pond*.

Meaningful Words (page 99)

1. A   2. B   3. B

Challenge: Check sentences to be sure contexts match the definitions chosen.

4. A   5. B   6. B

Challenge: Check sentences to be sure contexts match the definitions chosen.

Wacky Writing (page 100)

Students' responses should accurately answer each prompt and demonstrate understanding of the figurative phrase.

Say What? Extensions (page 101)

Check to see that students have completed two of the three activities.

Name _____ Date _____

Sea Life—Match That Figure!

Directions: Cut apart the definition cards. Glue each definition next to the correct phrase. Then, draw a picture to represent each figurative phrase.

Phrases	Definitions	Pictures
1. big fish in a small pond		
2. water under the bridge		
3. swim with the sharks		
4. fishing for a compliment		
5. still waters run deep		

doing or saying something so that someone says something nice about you	quiet people are often careful thinkers	something bad that happened in the past that cannot be changed	someone who is successful or important only in a small group	to be around or hang around bad or dangerous people

51625—Go Figure! Exploring Figurative Language

Sea Life—Choose That Figure!

Directions: Write the correct figure of speech in each sentence.

> » still waters run deep   » big fish in a small pond
>
> » swim with the sharks   » water under the bridge
>
> » fishing for a compliment

1. When Sarah wore her new party dress and spun around in front of the guests,

   it seemed like she was_____ .

2. Matsu started with a clean slate at his new school, so all the mistakes he made

   in the past were _____ .

3. My mother always told me to be careful who my friends were and to not

   " _____ ."

4. _____ in Miguel,

   so while he was quiet in class, he always answered questions thoughtfully.

Challenge: Write a sentence using the figure of speech not used above.

_____

_____

_____

_____

Sea Life—Meaningful Words

Directions: For each sentence, write the letter of the correct definition. Then, create your own sentence using the selected word.

big <u>fish</u> in a small pond	A. fish (noun): an aquatic animal with gills, fins, and scales B. fish (verb): to try to catch or get something

_____ 1. Tonight for dinner we are having fish and chips.

_____ 2. Carla was fishing for an answer from her mother about her birthday gift.

_____ 3. Growing up, I loved to fish with my grandfather.

Challenge: Choose a definition, and write a sentence using the word *fish*.

_____

_____

water under the <u>bridge</u>	A. bridge (noun): a structure providing a way to a river, road, or other gap B. bridge (verb): to make a connection between two structures or concepts

_____ 4. We took the bridge to the island so we could see the beach.

_____ 5. The newly built road bridged over the river.

_____ 6. The recorded music bridged the performers' singing.

Challenge: Choose a definition, and write a sentence using the word *bridge*.

_____

_____

Sea Life—Wacky Writing

Directions: Read and answer each prompt.

1. Describe a time where you were upset with someone but decided to forgive him or her because it was *water under the bridge.*

   _____

   _____

2. Explain why it would be a bad idea to *swim with the sharks* at school.

   _____

   _____

3. How might someone act when they have a new haircut and they are *fishing for a compliment?*

   _____

   _____

4. Describe a time when you felt like you were a *big fish in a small pond.*

   _____

   _____

   _____

5. Name three people you know who are really smart but often quiet because *still waters run deep.*

   _____

   _____

   _____

Sea Life—Say What? Extensions

Directions: Choose two activities to complete.

> » still waters run deep   » big fish in a small pond
>
> » swim with the sharks   » water under the bridge
>
> » fishing for a compliment

 ## Poetry Time

Choose one of the figures of speech. Then, create a short poem or rap with eight lines that would help someone younger than you understand the meaning of the figure of speech. You can use the definition, examples, and your own creativity to make it fun and interesting.

 ## Fishing for a Compliment

Everyone likes to be complimented sometimes, even if they aren't fishing for it! Using five small pieces of paper, write compliments to five people in your classroom and deliver them. Be sure to make the compliments something that will make them feel good when they read them.

 ## Hands in Motion

Find a partner. Take turns acting out each figure of speech using only your hands. You and your partner should also take turns trying to guess which one is being acted out.

big fish in a small pond

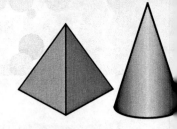

Figures of Speech

» get bent out of shape

» out of shape

» run circles around someone

» fair and square

» comes in all shapes and sizes

Overview

Students will enjoy learning about geometry-related idioms through the activities in this section. For detailed instructions on how to implement the activities in this lesson, see pages 8–10.

Materials

> copies of *Geometry—Match That Figure!* (page 103)
> copies of *Geometry—Choose That Figure!* (page 104)
> copies of *Geometry—Meaningful Words* (page 105)
> copies of *Geometry—Wacky Writing* (page 106)
> copies of *Geometry—Say What? Extensions* (page 107)
> scissors and glue
> index cards

Additional Figures of Speech

> size up
> square meal
> all squared away
> know every angle

Answer Key

Match That Figure! (page 103)

1. completely within the rules
2. to get angry or offended about something
3. to be available in a wide variety of things or types of people
4. to be more capable or work much harder than others doing the same task
5. not in good physical condition

Pictures will vary, but should show an understanding for each figure of speech.

Choose That Figure! (page 104)

1. fair and square
2. get bent out of shape
3. run circles around
4. out of shape

Challenge: Students create meaningful sentences with the figure of speech *comes in all shapes and sizes*.

Meaningful Words (page 105)

1. A   2. B   3. B

Challenge: Check sentences to be sure contexts match the definitions chosen.

4. B   5. A   6. A

Challenge: Check sentences to be sure contexts match the definitions chosen.

Wacky Writing (page 106)

Students' responses should accurately answer each prompt and demonstrate understanding of the figurative phrase.

Say What? Extensions (page 107)

Check to see that students have completed two of the three activities.

Geometry—Match That Figure!

Directions: Cut apart the definition cards. Glue each definition next to the correct phrase. Then, draw a picture to represent each figurative phrase.

Phrases	Definitions	Pictures
1. fair and square		
2. get bent out of shape		
3. comes in all shapes and sizes		
4. run circles around someone		
5. out of shape		

to be available in a wide variety of things or types of people	not in good physical condition	to get angry or offended about something	completely within the rules	to be more capable or work much harder than others doing the same task

Geometry—Choose That Figure!

Directions: Write the correct figure of speech in each sentence.

> » get bent out of shape   » out of shape
>
> » run circles around   » fair and square
>
> » comes in all shapes and sizes

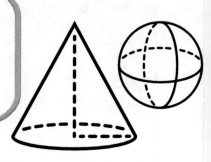

1. Although Justin was upset he lost the chess game, he knew Gavin had won

   the game _____ .

2. "Don't _____

   _____ just because you lost the baseball game," Eric said.

3. Julie was much better at working than Joe. In fact, she could _____

   _____him.

4. After stopping his exercise program and gaining weight, the man had a hard

   time walking up the stairs because he was _____ .

Challenge: Write a sentence using the figure of speech not used above.

_____

_____

_____

_____

Geometry—Meaningful Words

Directions: For each sentence, write the letter of the correct definition. Then, create your own sentence using the selected word.

out of <u>shape</u>	A. shape (noun): the design of the surface of an object B. shape (verb): to move around or change an object or someone's thinking

_____ 1. The shape of her new bedroom was a rectangle.

_____ 2. Dan tried to shape Bo's opinion about the movie by telling him how great it was.

_____ 3. Jamie and her family shaped the sand at the beach to look like a castle.

Challenge: Choose a definition, and write a sentence using the word *shape*.

_____

_____

comes in all shapes and <u>sizes</u>	A. size (noun): how big or small something is B. size (verb): to make something as large or small as you want it

_____ 4. Sophia's dress was too big, so she had it sized to fit her.

_____ 5. The size of Glenn's new office was twice the size of his old office.

_____ 6. Colette's feet grew two shoe sizes since she last bought shoes.

Challenge: Choose a definition, and write a sentence using the word *sizes*.

_____

_____

Geometry—Wacky Writing

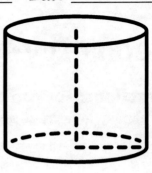

Directions: Read and answer each prompt.

1. Describe an activity you know you would probably win *fair and square* in a competition.

   _____

   _____

2. Name three things that would be hard for someone who was *out of shape* to do.

   _____

   _____

   _____

3. Name one thing, besides people, that *comes in all shapes and sizes.*

   _____

   _____

4. Describe one task you are so good at doing that you could *run circles around someone* doing the same task.

   _____

   _____

5. Describe something that really gets you *bent out of shape.*

   _____

   _____

Geometry—Say What? Extensions

Directions: Choose two activities to complete.

> » get bent out of shape
> » out of shape
> » run circles around someone
> » fair and square
> » comes in all shapes and sizes

 ## Comic Strip

Create a short four- to six-frame comic strip with sketches or simple pictures. Show the humor of one character using a figure of speech and the other character taking it literally.

 ## Short Story

Write a short description about something that recently happened to you using two of the figures of speech. Be sure the figures of speech are used correctly. Underline them when you are finished.

 ## Memory Game

Using five index cards, write each figure of speech on a separate card. Turn the cards over one at a time, and explain the definition of each phrase to a partner.

running circles around someone

51625—Go Figure! Exploring Figurative Language

Figures of Speech

» back to square one

» the third degree

» six of one and half dozen of the other

» two left feet

» on cloud nine

Overview

Students will enjoy learning about number-related idioms through the activities in this section. For detailed instructions on how to implement the activities in this lesson, see pages 8–10.

Materials

> copies of *Numbers—Match That Figure!* (page 109)
> copies of *Numbers—Choose That Figure!* (page 110)
> copies of *Numbers—Meaningful Words* (page 111)
> copies of *Numbers—Wacky Writing* (page 112)
> copies of *Numbers—Say What? Extensions* (page 113)
> scissors and glue

Additional Figures of Speech

> high five
> seventh heaven
> dress to the nines
> it takes two to tango
> two shakes of a lamb's tail
> stand on your own two feet
> two wrongs don't make a right
> two's company, three's a crowd

Answer Key

Match That Figure! (page 109)

1. having to go back to the beginning, often because of a mistake
2. being clumsy, especially with one's feet
3. to ask a person many questions in an intense, hostile way
4. two different ways of saying the same thing
5. feeling really good about something that happened

Pictures will vary, but should show an understanding for each figure of speech.

Choose That Figure! (page 110)

1. the third degree
2. two left feet
3. back to square one
4. six of one and half dozen of the other

Challenge: Students create meaningful sentences with the figure of speech *on cloud nine.*

Meaningful Words (page 111)

1. A   2. A   3. B

Challenge: Check sentences to be sure contexts match the definitions chosen.

4. B   5. A   6. A

Challenge: Check sentences to be sure contexts match the definitions chosen.

Wacky Writing (page 112)

Students' responses should accurately answer each prompt and demonstrate understanding of the figurative phrase.

Say What? Extensions (page 113)

Check to see that students have completed two of the three activities.

Numbers—Match That Figure! 13

Directions: Cut apart the definition cards. Glue each definition next to the correct phrase. Then, draw a picture to represent each figurative phrase.

Phrases	Definitions	Pictures
1. back to square one		
2. two left feet		
3. the third degree		
4. six of one and half dozen of the other		
5. on cloud nine		

two different ways of saying the same thing	feeling really good about something that happened	to ask a person many questions in an intense, hostile way	having to go back to the beginning, often because of a mistake	being clumsy, especially with one's feet

Numbers—Choose That Figure!

Directions: Write the correct figure of speech in each sentence.

> » back to square one   » two left feet
>
> » the third degree   » on cloud nine
>
> » six of one and half dozen of the other

1. Because Jill came home late from the movies, her mom gave her _____

   _____ , with questions about where she had been.

2. As Jamie tried to balance on the beam, he felt like he had _____

   _____ and fell off when he lost his balance.

3. Gloria lost the homework she was working on, so she had to go _____

   _____ and start all over again.

4. When Dad told me a different way to do the math problem, Mom said it was

   _____ because both ways produced the same answer.

Challenge: Write a sentence using the figure of speech not used above.

_____

_____

_____

_____

Numbers—Meaningful Words

Directions: For each sentence, write the letter of the correct definition. Then, create your own sentence using the selected word.

two left <u>feet</u>	A. foot (noun): the bottom part of the body beneath the leg with toes B. foot (noun): a unit of measure worth twelve inches

_____ 1. While we were moving, I dropped a heavy box on my foot.

_____ 2. When Jude put his foot in his shoe, he found a toy his baby brother had put in it.

_____ 3. My new coloring book was about a foot, with larger pictures in it.

Challenge: Choose a definition, and write a sentence using the word *feet*.

_____

_____

on <u>cloud</u> nine	A. cloud (noun): a collection of particles of water or ice formed together in the air B. cloud (verb): to confuse a person's mind or judgment

_____ 4. Miguel wanted to finish the project one way, but Beatrice clouded his thinking.

_____ 5. Waking up with dark clouds in the sky, we knew it might rain.

_____ 6. We could see many different shapes in the light, puffy clouds in the sky.

Challenge: Choose a definition, and write a sentence using the word *cloud*.

_____

_____

Numbers—Wacky Writing

Directions: Read and answer each prompt.

1. Describe a time when you felt like you had *two left feet*.

   _____

   _____

2. Describe a time you lost something or made a mistake and had to go *back to square one*.

   _____

   _____

3. Explain why a dad might give his son the *third degree*.

   _____

   _____

4. Describe what present you could get in the mail that would put you *on cloud nine*.

   _____

   _____

   _____

5. Explain something you can do equally well in more than one way—something that is *six of one and half dozen of the other*.

   _____

   _____

   _____

51625—Go Figure! Exploring Figurative Language

Numbers—Say What? Extensions

Directions: Choose two activities to complete.

> » back to square one   » two left feet
>
> » the third degree   » on cloud nine
>
> » six of one and half dozen of the other

 Sing Me a Song

With a partner, write a simple song to a familiar tune. Include at least one of the figures of speech in your song. Share your song by singing it or reading the lyrics aloud like a poem.

Read All About It!

With a partner, pretend you work for a news organization and have to write one paragraph about something that happened in your town. The story should contain at least two of this week's figures of speech.

 Mime Time

Take turns with your partner or group members acting out all five of the figures of speech. You may only use body language and gestures to act out the clues. You may not use your voice!

on cloud nine

51625—Go Figure! Exploring Figurative Language

Figures of Speech

» there aren't enough hours in the day

» April showers bring May flowers

» an apple a day keeps the doctor away

» slow as molasses in January

» all in a day's work

Overview

Students will enjoy learning about calendar-related idioms through the activities in this section. For detailed instructions on how to implement the activities in this lesson, see pages 8–10.

Materials

> copies of *Calendar Time—Match That Figure!* (page 115)

> copies of *Calendar Time—Choose That Figure!* (page 116)

> copies of *Calendar Time—Meaningful Words* (page 117)

> copies of *Calendar Time—Wacky Writing* (page 118)

> copies of *Calendar Time—Say What? Extensions* (page 119)

> scissors and glue

> index cards

Additional Figures of Speech

> 24/7

> have a field day

> a month of Sundays

> every dog has its day

> tomorrow is another day

> knee high by the Fourth of July

> won't give someone the time of day

Answer Key

Match That Figure! (page 115)

1. sometimes something unpleasant or difficult brings a pleasant reward
2. very slow moving
3. doing little things regularly will help prevent big problems in the future
4. being very busy with a project
5. doing what is expected or normal

Pictures will vary, but should show an understanding for each figure of speech.

Choose That Figure! (page 116)

1. April showers bring May flowers
2. there weren't enough hours in the day
3. slow as molasses in January
4. an apple a day keeps the doctor away

Challenge: Students create meaningful sentences with the figure of speech *all in a day's work.*

Meaningful Words (page 117)

1. B   2. A   3. C

Challenge: Check sentences to be sure contexts match the definitions chosen.

4. A   5. B   6. A

Challenge: Check sentences to be sure contexts match the definitions chosen.

Wacky Writing (page 118)

Students' responses should accurately answer each prompt and demonstrate understanding of the figurative phrase.

Say What? Extensions (page 119)

Check to see that students have completed two of the three activities.

24

Calendar Time—Match That Figure!

Directions: Cut apart the definition cards. Glue each definition next to the correct phrase. Then, draw a picture to represent each figurative phrase.

Phrases	Definitions	Pictures
1. April showers bring May flowers		
2. slow as molasses in January		
3. an apple a day keeps the doctor away		
4. there aren't enough hours in the day		
5. all in a day's work		

very slow moving	doing what is expected or normal	sometimes something unpleasant or difficult brings a pleasant reward	being very busy with a project	doing little things regularly will help prevent big problems in the future

Calendar Time—Choose That Figure!

Directions: Write the correct figure of speech in each sentence.

> » there weren't enough hours in the day » slow as molasses in January
>
> » April showers bring May flowers » all in a day's work
>
> » an apple a day keeps the doctor away

1. The children had worked hard planting the tomato seeds early in the season

    to get tomatoes later because _____

    _____ .

2. Rena felt like _____

    _____ when she was only able to complete three of her five chores.

3. Even though he is trying hard, that turtle is moving as _____

    _____ .

4. Exercising and eating well each day will help keep you healthy because

    _____ .

Challenge: Write a sentence using the figure of speech not used above.

_____

_____

_____

Calendar Time—Meaningful Words

Directions: For each sentence, write the letter of the correct definition. Then, create your own sentence using the selected word.

April <u>showers</u> bring May flowers	A. shower (noun): a brief fall of rain
	B. shower (verb): to clean yourself with falling water
	C. shower (noun): a party to celebrate a wedding or a baby

_____ 1. After football practice, Jake really needed to shower.

_____ 2. Before bed, mom let us go outside and play in the shower of rain.

_____ 3. As a gift for the shower, Marty made a baby blanket.

Challenge: Choose a definition, and write a sentence using the word *showers*.

_____

_____

| an apple a day keeps the <u>doctor</u> away | A. doctor (noun): a person who is licensed to practice medicine and help sick people |
| | B. doctor (verb): to treat someone's sickness or something that is hurt |

_____ 4. Gabby felt sick all day, so her mom took her to the doctor.

_____ 5. Gloria had to doctor her ankle after twisting it playing volleyball.

_____ 6. The doctor checked the little boy and found that he had a fever.

Challenge: Choose a definition, and write a sentence using the word *doctor*.

_____

_____

Calendar Time—Wacky Writing

Directions: Read and answer each prompt.

1. Since *April showers bring May flowers*, describe one unpleasant or difficult thing that you would have to do now to get something good later.

   _____

   _____

2. Since an *apple a day keeps the doctor away*, name three things you can do each day to stay healthy.

   _____

   _____

3. Describe three things that are *all in a day's work* for a parent.

   _____

   _____

4. Describe a fun activity that would make you feel like *there aren't enough hours in the day*.

   _____

   _____

   _____

5. Name two liquids or foods that are *slow as molasses in January* when you pour them.

   _____

   _____

51625—Go Figure! Exploring Figurative Language   © *Shell Education*

Calendar Time—Say What? Extensions

Directions: Choose two activities to complete.

> » there aren't enough hours in the day » slow as molasses in January
>
> » April showers bring May flowers » all in a day's work
>
> » an apple a day keeps the doctor away

 Example and Non-Example

Choose one figure of speech. Then, write two sentences using the figure of speech appropriately, and two using the figure of speech incorrectly. Read the four sentences to a partner, and have him or her figure out which two sentences are good examples and which two sentences are non-examples.

◄► Matching Game

Create a matching game with a partner. Using 10 index cards, write each figure of speech on one card and your own definition for each phrase on another card. Mix up all the cards. Time how long it takes you to match each figure of speech with its definition. Have your partner try to beat your time. Each person goes twice to see who can achieve the fastest time.

 Critical Thinking

Create a piece of artwork with symbols and pictures that represent the meaning of one of the figures of speech. You may not use any words in the piece. Share your picture with a partner or group to see if they can guess which figure of speech you chose.

an apple a day keeps the doctor away

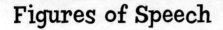

Money

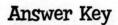

Figures of Speech

» look like a million bucks
» time is money
» put in my two cents
» not made of money
» money doesn't grow on trees

Overview

Students will enjoy learning about money-related idioms through the activities in this section. For detailed instructions on how to implement the activities in this lesson, see pages 8–10.

Materials

> copies of *Money—Match That Figure!* (page 121)
> copies of *Money—Choose That Figure!* (page 122)
> copies of *Money—Meaningful Words* (page 123)
> copies of *Money—Wacky Writing* (page 124)
> copies of *Money—Say What? Extensions* (page 125)
> scissors and glue

Additional Figures of Speech

> penny pincher
> a pretty penny
> pressed for money
> fork out some money
> it takes money to make money

Answer Key

Match That Figure! (page 121)

1. earning money can be hard work, so be careful how you spend it
2. wasting time may cause you to lose out on the opportunity to make money
3. not having an endless supply of money
4. something that is very attractive to view
5. giving your own opinion about something even when not asked

Pictures will vary, but should show an understanding for each figure of speech.

Choose That Figure! (page 122)

1. money doesn't grow on trees
2. not made of money
3. looked like a million bucks
4. time is money

Challenge: Students create meaningful sentences with the figure of speech *put in my two cents*.

Meaningful Words (page 123)

1. A 2. C 3. B

Challenge: Check sentences to be sure contexts match the definitions chosen.

4. A 5. B 6. A

Challenge: Check sentences to be sure contexts match the definitions chosen.

Wacky Writing (page 124)

Students' responses should accurately answer each prompt and demonstrate understanding of the figurative phrase.

Say What? Extensions (page 125)

Check to see that students have completed two of the three activities.

51625—Go Figure! Exploring Figurative Language

Money—Match That Figure!

Directions: Cut apart the definition cards. Glue each definition next to the correct phrase. Then, draw a picture to represent each figurative phrase.

Phrases	Definitions	Pictures
1. money doesn't grow on trees		
2. time is money		
3. not made of money		
4. look like a million bucks		
5. put in your two cents		

something that is very attractive to view	earning money can be hard work, so be careful how you spend it	giving your opinion about something even when not asked	wasting time may cause you to lose out on the opportunity to make money	not having an endless supply of money

Money—Choose That Figure!

Directions: Write the correct figure of speech in each sentence.

> » looked like a million bucks » time is money
>
> » put in my two cents » not made of money
>
> » money doesn't grow on trees

1. Dad said we had to carefully save for our trip because "_____

   _____ ."

2. Lindsey's family is _____

   _____, so she had to take out a loan to go to college.

3. Gabby _____

   _____ when she walked down the stairs in her new dress.

4. Dad came home from work late because _____

   _____ , and he had to finish working on a big project.

Challenge: Write a sentence using the figure of speech not used above.

_____

_____

_____

_____

Money—Meaningful Words

Directions: For each sentence, write the letter of the correct definition. Then, create your own sentence using the selected word.

looks like a million <u>bucks</u>	**A.** buck (noun): a male deer
	B. buck (noun): another word for money; a dollar
	C. buck (verb): to get off or go against

_____ 1. From the television program we learned what life is like for a buck.

_____ 2. The protesters bucked the idea of a wage freeze and went on strike.

_____ 3. Shelby earned three bucks for babysitting her neighbor's cat.

Challenge: Choose a definition, and write a sentence using the word *bucks*.

_____

_____

| money doesn't <u>grow</u> on trees | **A.** grow (verb): to increase in size |
| | **B.** grow (verb): to become older |

_____ 4. It was hard waiting for the apple tree that we planted to grow.

_____ 5. Growing up usually means more responsibility.

_____ 6. Our class watched the plants grow as the year went on.

Challenge: Choose a definition, and write a sentence using the word *grow*.

_____

_____

Name _____ Date _____

Money—Wacky Writing

Directions: Read and answer each prompt.

1. Explain why your parents might tell you they are *not made of money*.

   _____

   _____

2. Name an event you might attend that would cause you to dress in fine clothes because you want to *look like a million bucks*.

   _____

   _____

3. Describe two things you could do to be careful with your money since *money doesn't grow on trees*.

   _____

   _____

4. If *time is money*, describe something that would be good to get done quickly.

   _____

   _____

   _____

5. Describe a time when nobody asked for your opinion, but you *put in your two cents* anyway.

   _____

   _____

   _____

Money—Say What? Extensions

Directions: Choose two activities to complete.

> » looked like a million bucks   » time is money
>
> » put in my two cents   » not made of money
>
> » money doesn't grow on trees

$ Look like a Million Bucks

Describe and sketch the perfect way for you to look if you were going to meet your favorite celebrity. What would you wear? What accessories would you have? How would you do your hair?

Hands in Motion

Find a partner. Take turns acting out each figure of speech using only your hands. You and your partner should also take turns trying to guess which one is being acted out.

Say It, Don't Spray It!

Work with the whole class to write and tell a story that includes all five figures of speech. One person begins the story. Then, each person takes a turn adding an idea to the story. Continue the story until all figures of speech have been used and the story comes to an end.

money doesn't grow on trees

Figures of Speech

» turn back the clock

» race against the clock

» time flies when you're having fun

» have the time of your life

» no time like the present

Overview

Students will enjoy learning about time-related idioms through the activities in this section. For detailed instructions on how to implement the activities in this lesson, see pages 8–10.

Materials

> copies of *Time—Match That Figure!* (page 127)
> copies of *Time—Choose That Figure!* (page 128)
> copies of *Time—Meaningful Words* (page 129)
> copies of *Time—Wacky Writing* (page 130)
> copies of *Time—Say What? Extensions* (page 131)
> scissors and glue

Additional Figures of Speech

> top of the hour
> beat the clock
> bottom of the hour
> at the eleventh hour
> all hours of the night
> a time and place for everything

Answer Key

Match That Figure! (page 127)
1. time seems to go by very quickly if you are doing something you enjoy
2. having a wonderful experience that will make good memories
3. trying to rush to get a task done that has a time deadline
4. start doing something now instead of putting it off to a later time
5. wanting to go back in time and do something differently

Pictures will vary, but should show an understanding for each figure of speech.

Choose That Figure! (page 128)
1. racing against the clock
2. time flies when you're having fun
3. had the time of our lives
4. turn back the clock

Challenge: Students create meaningful sentences with the figure of speech *no time like the present*.

Meaningful Words (page 129)
1. A   2. A   3. B
Challenge: Check sentences to be sure contexts match the definitions chosen.
4. A   5. B   6. B
Challenge: Check sentences to be sure contexts match the definitions chosen.

Wacky Writing (page 130)
Students' responses should accurately answer each prompt and demonstrate understanding of the figurative phrase.

Say What? Extensions (page 131)
Check to see that students have completed two of the three activities.

Name _____ Date _____

Time—Match That Figure!

Directions: Cut apart the definition cards. Glue each definition next to the correct phrase. Then, draw a picture to represent each figurative phrase.

Phrases	Definitions	Pictures
1. time flies when you're having fun		
2. have the time of your life		
3. race against the clock		
4. no time like the present		
5. turn back the clock		

start doing something now instead of putting it off to a later time	wanting to go back in time and do something differently	trying to rush to get a task done that has a time deadline	time seems to go by very quickly if you are doing something you enjoy	having a wonderful experience that will make good memories

51625—Go Figure! Exploring Figurative Language

Time—Choose That Figure!

Directions: Write the correct figure of speech in each sentence.

> » turn back the clock   » had the time of our lives
>
> » racing against the clock   » no time like the present
>
> » time flies when you're having fun

1. The class was _____

   _____ to get the classroom clean before the principal arrived.

2. Joyce exclaimed, " _____

   _____ !" when she realized it was already time for the carnival to close.

3. We _____

   _____ at our family reunion and created great memories.

4. The mom watched her youngest child go off to college and wished she could

   _____ to when he was a little boy.

Challenge: Write a sentence using the figure of speech not used above.

_____

_____

_____

_____

Time—Meaningful Words

Directions: For each sentence, write the letter of the correct definition. Then, create your own sentence using the selected word.

<u>race</u> against the clock	**A.** race (noun): a contest of speed in a sport or other competition **B.** race (verb): to engage in a contest of speed in a sport or other competition

_____ 1. The puppies were all lined up, and the race was on!

_____ 2. The race for school president was between a brother and a sister.

_____ 3. Racing down the hill, the children all began to laugh.

Challenge: Choose a definition, and write a sentence using the word *race*.

_____

_____

no time like the <u>present</u>	**A.** present (noun): at this time or now **B.** present (noun): a gift given from one person to another

_____ 4. At present, our principal is Mr. Liu, and he started working here this year.

_____ 5. For his birthday, I gave my cousin a skateboard as a present.

_____ 6. After I got the invitation, I knew I wanted to get her a present for her party.

Challenge: Choose a definition, and write a sentence using the word *present*.

_____

_____

Time—Wacky Writing

Directions: Read and answer each prompt.

1. If you could *turn back the clock,* to what time in your life would you return? Explain why.

   _____

   _____

2. Explain a time when you had to *race against the clock* to finish a task on time.

   _____

   _____

3. Describe an experience that you would call *the time of your life.*

   _____

   _____

4. Describe an activity that makes you feel that *time flies when you're having fun.*

   _____

   _____

5. Explain why your teacher might tell you that there is *no time like the present* to start your homework.

   _____

   _____

Time—Say What? Extensions

Directions: Choose two activities to complete.

> » turn back the clock   » had the time of our lives
>
> » racing against the clock   » no time like the present
>
> » time flies when you're having fun

 ## Tell Me a Tale

Create a fairy tale with a small group. The story should be funny, short, and use at least two figures of speech. Each person can only say one word at a time to tell the story. For example, the first person might say "once." Then, the next person would say "upon." The third person would say "a," and the fourth person would say "time."

 ## Figurative and Literal

Choose one figure of speech. Using a sheet of paper folded in half, write "literal" and "figurative" at the top of each side. Under "literal," draw your interpretation of the literal meaning of the figure of speech. Under "figurative," draw your interpretation of the figurative meaning of the figure of speech. Write the figure of speech on the back of your paper.

 ## Poetry Time

Choose one of the figures of speech. Then, create a short poem or rap with eight lines that would help someone younger than you understand the meaning of the figure of speech. You can use the definition, examples, and your own creativity to make it fun and interesting.

racing against the clock

References Cited

Blachowicz, Camille, and Peter J. Fisher. 2014. *Teaching Vocabulary in All Classrooms*. 5th ed. New York, NY: Pearson.

Harris, Theodore Lester, and Richard E. Hodges. 1995. *The Literacy Dictionary: The Vocabulary of Reading and Writing*. Newark, DE: International Reading Association.

National Reading Panel. 2000. *The Report of the National Reading Panel*. Washington, DC: US Department of Education.

Additional Resources

Teachers can use the classroom resource list below to learn more about how to incorporate figurative language instruction into the classroom.

"Books with Figurative Language." *This Reading Mama*. Accessed August 9, 2016. http://thisreadingmama.com/books-figurative-language/.

Colston, Herbert L., and Melissa S. Kuiper. 2002. "Figurative Language Development Research and Popular Children's Literature: Why We Should Know 'Where the Wild Things Are.'" *Metaphor and Symbol* 17 (1): 27–43.

Hazelton, Rebecca. 2015. "Learning About Figurative Language: How to Use Simile and Metaphor Like a Boss." *Poetry Foundation*. April 13, 2015. http://www.poetryfoundation.org/learning/article/250298.

"Homepage—ReadWriteThink." *Readwritethink.org*. Accessed August 9, 2016. http://www.readwritethink.org/.

Palmer, Barbara C., Vikki S. Shackelford, and Judith T. Leclere. 2006. "Bridging Two Worlds: Reading Comprehension, Figurative Language Instruction, and the English Language Learner." *Journal of Adolescent and Adult Literacy* 50 (4): 258–267.

Petrosky, Anthony R. 1980. "The Inferences We Make: Children and Literature." *Language Arts* 57 (2): 149–156.

Rasinski, Timothy. 2008. *Idioms and Other English Expressions: 1–3*. Huntington Beach, CA: Shell Education.

Rasinski, Timothy. 2008. *Idioms and Other English Expressions: 4–6*. Huntington Beach, CA: Shell Education.

Rasinski, Timothy, and Melissa Cheesman Smith. 2014. *Vocabulary Ladders: Understanding Word Nuances*. Huntington, CA: Teacher Created Materials.

Rasinski, Timothy, and Jerry Zutell. 2010. *Essential Strategies for Word Study: Effective Methods for Improving Decoding, Spelling, and Vocabulary*. New York, NY: Scholastic.

Spears, Richard A. 2006. *A Dictionary of American Idioms*. 4th ed. New York, NY: McGraw-Hill.

"The Best Children's Books!" *The Best Children's Books!* Accessed August 11, 2016. http://thebestchildrensbooks.org/.

"The Idiom Connection." *The Idiom Connection*. Accessed August 9, 2016. http://www.idiomconnection.com/.

Vasquez, Anete. 2005. "Literary Analysis 101." *The English Journal* 94 (6): 97–100.

Zutell, Jerry. 2016. *Word Wisdom: Unlocking Vocabulary in Context*. Columbus, OH: Zaner-Bloser.

Check It Out!

Websites

Teachers can use the websites below to learn more about how to incorporate figurative language instruction into the classroom.

Figurativelanguage.net

This website offers an in-depth explanation of figurative language: alliteration, hyperbole, imagery, irony, metaphor, onomatopoeia, oxymoron, personification, and similes.

Idiomconnection.com

This idiom website contains a comprehensive list of idioms organized alphabetically and by themes, such as animal, body, color, and food. Each section concludes with a comprehensive quiz, which tests students' knowledge of the idioms in the section.

Literarydevices.net

This website contains a comprehensive list of over 100 literary devices. Each device is coupled with multiple examples and a short section that explains the function of each literary device.

Readwritethink.org

This website is devoted to English language learning and literacy. Here, educators can find classroom and after-school resources on how to teach idioms to students in grades 3–5.

Thebestchildrensbooks.org

This site, created by three teachers, has hundreds of books listed for school-aged children. Educators can find books on many of the figurative language staples, including idioms, similes, and onomatopoeia.

Thisreadingmama.com

Becky Spence, a homeschooling-blogger-mom, compiles a detailed list of books that contain and teach figurative language. Each book on her list has a detailed explanation of what type(s) of figurative language can be found in the book and some of the themes present in the book.

Children's Books with Figurative Language

The list below offers great examples of figurative language for students across all grade levels.

Arnold, Tedd. 2003. *More Parts*. New York, NY: Puffin Books.

———. 2007. *Even More Parts*. New York, NY: Puffin Books.

Brinckloe, Julie. 1986. *Fireflies!* New York, NY: Aladdin.

Burton, Virginia Lee. 1978. *The Little House*. New York, NY: HMH Books for Young Readers.

Cleary, Brian P. 2009. *Skin Like Milk, Hair of Silk: What are Similes and Metaphors?* Minneapolis, MN: Millbrook Press.

Floca, Brian. 2013. *Locomotive*. New York, NY: Atheneum Books.

Frazee, Marla. 2006. *Roller Coaster*. New York, NY: HMH Books for Young Readers.

Gobel, Paul. 1993. *The Girl Who Loved Wild Horses*. New York, NY: Aladdin.

Gwynne, Fred. 1988. *A Chocolate Moose for Dinner*. New York, NY: Aladdin.

———. 1988. *The King Who Rained*. New York, NY: Aladdin.

Leedy, Loren. 2003. *There's a Frog in My Throat: 440 Animal Sayings a Little Bird Told Me*. New York, NY: Holiday House.

———. 2009. *Crazy like a Fox: A Simile Story*. New York, NY: Holiday House.

Parish, Peggy. 1963. *Amelia Bedelia*. New York, NY: HarperCollins.

Piven, Hanoch. 2007. *My Dog is as Smelly as Dirty Socks: And Other Funny Family Portraits*. New York, NY: Schwartz and Wade.

———. 2010. *My Best Friend is as Sharp as a Pencil*. New York, NY: Random House.

———. 2013. *My Dog is as Smelly as Dirty Socks*. New York, NY: Random House.

Potter, Beatrix. 1902. *The Complete Tales of Peter the Rabbit*. New York, NY: Penguin.

Prelutsky, Jack. 1999. *20th Century Children's Poetry Treasury*. New York, NY: Knopf Books for Young Readers.

Teague, Mark. 2004. *Pigsty*. New York, NY: Scholastic.

Terban, Marvin. 1983. *In a Pickle*. New York, NY: Houghton Mifflin.

Tresselt, Alvin. 1988. *White Snow, Bright Snow*. New York, NY: HarperCollins.

Silverstein, Shel. 1964. *The Giving Tree*. New York, NY: HarperCollins.

———. 1974. *Where the Sidewalk Ends*. New York, NY: HarperCollins.

Steig, William. 1969. *Sylvester and the Magic Pebble*. New York, NY: Aladdin.

Van Allsburg, Chris. 1985. *The Polar Express*. New York, NY: HMH Books for Young Readers.

———. 1988. *Two Bad Ants*. New York, NY: HMH Books for Young Readers.

Weston, Carol. 2015. *Taco Cat*. Naperville, IL: Sourcebooks Jabberwocky.

Winter, Jeanette. 1988. *Follow the Drinking Gourd*. New York, NY: Random House.

Wood, Audrey. 1990. *Quick as a Cricket*. Auburn, ME: Child's Play International Limited.

Yolen, Jane. 1987. *Owl Moon*. New York, NY: Philomel Books.

Young, Ed. 2002. *Seven Blind Mice*. New York, NY: Puffin Books.

51625—Go Figure! Exploring Figurative Language